SANDRINE'S PARIS

To my mind, what makes Paris so magical is precisely what escapes us about it. The things that are impossible to translate ...

SANDRINE'S

A cultural history of the world's most romantic city

PARIS

Sandrine Voillet

Edited by Georgina Oliver

BBC
BOOKS

CONTENTS

AN ATMOSPHERIC MOSAIC

The Canal Saint-Martin, with its succession of locks and bridges, exudes Parisian atmosphere and ranks among the most evocative settings in the capital of haute couture and art de vivre.

LEFT Ill-fated lovers in Marcel Carné's *Hôtel du Nord* (1938). The film re-creates the atmosphere of *Paname* (French slang for 'Paris'), before the Second World War.
OPPOSITE Paris seen from the slopes of Montmartre: a mosaic of grey rooftops and modern constructions, including the Tour Montparnasse skyscraper. Art lovers will spot two of the capital's principal museums, the Louvre, to the left of the giant Ferris wheel in the Tuileries Gardens, and the Musée d'Orsay (to its right).

'Atmosphère, atmosphère...' The most famous phrase in the history of French cinema (from Marcel Carné's *Hôtel du Nord*, 1938) springs instantly to mind when I stroll along the banks of the Canal Saint-Martin in Paris's 10th arrondissement. To a film-loving art historian like myself, this quaintly picturesque yet trendy quarter, featuring a succession of locks and bridges, exudes Parisian atmosphere. At once steeped in history and eminently fashionable, it ranks among the most evocative settings in the capital of haute couture and *art de vivre* (the art of living). Thinking about what crystallizes the atmosphere of Paris, I wonder whether the essence of the city could be the contrast between the natural effervescence of its café-frequenting population and the apparent determination of its various architects through the ages to keep this ebullience under control – literally to canalize or channel all that unbridled creative energy. As I see it, the tension between the passionate nature of its inhabitants and the imposing elegance of its highly structured architecture – itself the work of impas-sioned creative spirits – is what sparks inventiveness and change in the city I began to explore as a student at the Ecole du Louvre.

Recently renovated by the city authorities, the rather yuppie 10th arrondissement has retained a village-like aura, echoing the bucolic charm it must have possessed three centuries ago, before Louis XIV first entertained the idea of building an urban water-way in one of his kingdom's rural suburbs. Napoleon I persisted with this ingenious engineering project, designed to supply the capital with drinking water, and the Canal Saint-Martin was eventually completed in 1825. Here you can eat in old-style bistros, such as L'Atmosphère at 49 rue Lucien-Sampaix.

At 102 quai de Jemmapes is a cinematographic landmark, the Hôtel du Nord, for ever linked with Marcel Carné's great screen drama of the same name. Now reinvented as a convivial restaurant, it stages shows that spotlight English-speaking stand-up comedians. Developers attempted to acquire the premises, hoping to transform this officially registered

historical monument, saved from demolition in 1986, into a fast-food outlet. That, however, is another story.

Although fans of the film will inevitably experience a slight frisson when they walk past the place bearing its name, Carné's monument to 1930s' poetic realism was not actually filmed there. *Hôtel du Nord* was shot in Boulogne-Billancourt on Paris's western outskirts, in studios that are no less legendary than the film itself. This is where art director Alexandre

Trauner reproduced the atmosphere of *Paname* (French slang for 'Paris') before the Second World War.

Social Insights

To my mind, what makes Paris so magical is precisely what escapes us about it. The things that are impossible to translate. As the title of Sofia Coppola's celebrated 2003 film *Lost in Translation* suggests, a city's inner mechanisms are as mysterious to

ABOVE A City of Light in the daytime, our capital turns into a City of Lights after dusk as Gustave Eiffel's tower looms over Paris by night.

How do I visualize my city? Perhaps as a mosaic of atmospheres asserting their distinctive identities within the constraints of elegant avenues, ancient ramparts and freshly defined boundaries.

outsiders as the chemistry that attracts potential lovers.

There's a fun series of pocket-sized guidebooks called Parigramme that I enjoy flicking through when I come across them in a bookshop. They focus on unexpected themes with a Paris connection. 'Real' Parisians, not just tourists and sightseers, read them because they're filled with amusing anecdotes and historical details. One of the books has an irresistible title: *Où s'embrasser à Paris* (Where to Kiss in Paris). It lists several Seine- and canal-side spots, and includes an itinerary for romantic bikers. From 2 p.m. to 6 p.m. on Sundays the streets linking the Canal Saint-Martin's charming locks become a pollution-free, no-go zone for cars, and a haven for cyclists and skaters, many of whom are affluent, environment-conscious 'bobos'. This term was coined by the American writer David Brooks in his book *Bobos in Paradise: The New*

ABOVE May '68. Protestors hurl paving stones amid tear gas and assemble on the boulevard Saint-Michel, barricaded behind wrecked cars. Le Luxembourg is now one of Paris's popular *cafés-philo*, hosting weekly philosophical debates.

Upper Class and How They Got There (2000) to identify a rising generation of information-age 'bourgeois bohemians' with spending power. And although not everybody in Paris has read the French translation, *Les Bobos*, everybody knows that the city's *quartiers populaires* (working-class districts) have been taken over by bobos who have converted the disused tanneries, paper mills and potteries in these increasingly gentrified neighbourhoods into stylish lofts.

Another word worth investigating when examining Paris's social make-up is 'bourgeois'. Formerly used merely to refer to the burghers of towns or districts who were neither working class nor farmers, aristocrats or clerics, the term nowadays conjures up visions of a comfortably prosperous category of bon vivants, middle- and upper middle-class Parisians whose conventional dress codes and sense of decorum are either mocked or envied. Although they are often presented as arbiters of good taste, the notion of *goût bourgeois* (bourgeois taste) is perceived as being a bit pejorative, evoking plain cooking, homely clothing and cosy interiors, in other words, an unadventurous lifestyle. This is a curious paradox, considering that many of them are entrepreneurs. But there's nothing new about this attitude towards the bourgeoisie.

In 1670, more than a century before the French Revolution, the playwright Molière caricatured the naive attitude of Monsieur Jourdain, a nouveau-riche bourgeois who was determined to 'act noble', in his celebrated comedy *Le Bourgeois Gentilhomme* (The Bourgeois Gentleman), while in May 1968 students took to the streets, installing barricades and hurling paving stones, largely to rebel against the rigidity of a society governed by petit-bourgeois values.

Today the middle classes are frequently ridiculed on satirical television shows that continue to wield a typically French brand of whiplash humour that is somewhat reminiscent of the mordant wit of the Versailles courtiers in Patrice Leconte's acclaimed film *Ridicule* (1996).

Not unlike the milk that is a basic ingredient of *café au lait*, France's traditional breakfast drink, Parisians tend to be ever ready to reach boiling point, protesting when the means of ascending the social ladder appears to be blocked. This was demonstrated by the riot scenes of November 2005, broadcast worldwide, when young activists drew attention to the lack of flexibility in France's educational system and its restrictive job market, which is traditionally dominated by the alumni of the *grandes écoles*. These elitist, university-level establishments are rarely attended by the children of immigrants, born in *cités de banlieue* (suburban estates) situated beyond the Périphérique, the circular roadway that marks the capital's limits, much as ramparts used to surround fortified strongholds.

Efforts have been made to combat the sense of injustice that surrounds France's scholastic elitism. Sciences Po (the nickname for a *grande école* that specializes in political science) and ESSEC (a leading business school) have both experimented with positive discrimination in favour of students from Zeps (Zones d'Éducation Prioritaire), disadvantaged urban areas that qualify for priority programmes and resources. Nevertheless, the emergence of educational inequalities, attributed to social, racial and academic segregation, continues to be a major issue.

Architecture and Atmosphere

Prohibitive property prices and rising rents have turned living in the city centre into something of a privilege, accentuating the widespread impression that Parisians are obliged to struggle to survive in a *société à deux vitesse* (two-gear society), where average citizens find it hard to keep up with those in the fast lane. In the early 1970s a number of prominent young architects, aware that having access to beauty on a daily basis was rapidly becoming the ultimate luxury, looked into the idea of producing low-cost accommodation that took this into account. Breaking away from the dehumanized concrete constructions of a good many of their predecessors, they relied on contrasting materials in subtle juxtapositions and varied proportions (different-sized doors, windows, arches and curves) to create buildings with a poetic dimension.

In this spirit, Christian de Portzamparc built a block of affordable HLM flats (HLM stands for *habitations à loyer modéré* – low-rent homes). Named after a street on the original site, the Hautes Formes housing scheme (located in the Italie-Tolbiac district, better known these days as one of Paris's two thriving Chinatowns) paved the way for larger-scale realizations that attach importance to the atmosphere of a building.

The Age of Enlightenment

In French history books, the Age of Enlightenment is associated with the eighteenth century, known as the Siècle des lumières (Century of Lights) – an era marked by great thinkers who exchanged ideas in the *salon*s, coffee houses and clubs that emerged during the period of political effervescence that led to the Revolution.

Among these leading lights, Voltaire epitomizes the revolutionary spirit of the Siècle des lumières. This prolific, sharp-witted author, influenced by the empiricist views of the English philosopher John Locke, returned from three years of exile in England with a fresh outlook. In 1764, he published a *Dictionnaire philosophique* (Philosophical Dictionary), presenting controversial topics – such as government, freedom of speech, literature and religion – in a new light. Voltaire's dictionary was part of a bigger picture. It was based on a series of essays previously penned for Diderot's celebrated *Encyclopédie*, an encyclopedia devoted to science, arts and crafts whose list of contributors reads like a 'who's who' of the French Enlightenment, from Jean-Jacques Rousseau to Montesquieu. These free spirits shared a common goal: to change the way people think. They formed a 'republic of letters', gathering at the homes of high-society *salonnières* with a talent for bringing enlightened minds together.

ABOVE A contemporary portrait of Voltaire in his study by an unknown artist.

A star in this extremely competitive domain, which puts commissions out to tender, is the uncompromising architect Jean Nouvel, who has created a series of new-style landmarks that have changed the face of Paris. His latest building with a cultural mission is the Musée du quai Branly, which is dedicated to the arts and civilizations of Africa, Asia, Oceania and the Americas. Anyone walking across the Pont de l'Alma towards the Eiffel Tower, en route from Alma-Marceau, the Métro stop for the unofficial memorial to 'Ladee Dee' (the late Princess of Wales), simply cannot miss its leafy façade, with its vertical garden by Patrick Blanc. The memorial to the princess, incidentally, is a bronze replica of the Statue of Liberty's flame, donated to the City of Paris by the *International Herald Tribune* newspaper as a tribute to Franco-American friendship.

Likewise conceived by Jean Nouvel, the Fondation Cartier contemporary-art collection on boulevard Raspail certainly has atmosphere in abundance. After seeing its avant-garde exhibitions, visitors like to linger in its tranquil inner garden, which is visible from the street. The objective of this airy, multi-storey glass and metal space? According to the architect, 'Total dematerialization'. It's so transparent that we forget what it's made of.

OPPOSITE AND TOP
Jean Nouvel's bold design for the Musée du quai Branly.
ABOVE En route to the new museum, sightseers gather around Paris's unofficial memorial to the late Diana, Princess of Wales – a bronze replica of the Statue of Liberty's flame that was donated to the City of Paris by the *International Herald Tribune*.

Abstract motifs on the wall overlooking the south-facing courtyard garden of the Institut du Monde Arabe recall the elaborate latticework of Islamic art.

There is more translucent glass at the Institut du Monde Arabe (Institute of the Arab World), where the Nouvel–Architecture Studio team worked in tandem to create a multi-purpose environment devoted to Franco-Arabic cultural exchanges. Compared to a giant Venetian blind by some early observers, the wall overlooking its south-facing courtyard garden operates like a camera lens – abstract motifs recalling the elaborate latticework of Islamic art alternate as its artificial irises react to the sunlight. One feature that unites the practical with the symbolic is the narrow slit that separates the museum part of the building from the library: this is orientated in the direction of Notre-Dame Cathedral, representing the desire to establish an ongoing dialogue between monuments with different historical and spiritual roots.

Despite the self-avowed errors of certain town planners, under pressure to provide the city's periphery with cheap, high-rise housing for incoming workers during the three-decade economic boom France enjoyed after the Second World War, present-day Paris strikes me, on balance, as overwhelmingly alluring. More than a postcard-pretty face, it has made the leap to modern metropolis. Yet, on the whole, its decision-makers' worst instincts seem to have been held in check. Why? In part, this is thanks to stringent legislation intended to protect the capital's old buildings, and partly, of course, it is because of the sheer beauty of the monuments and architectural schemes successive sovereigns, prelates and political leaders have envisioned from one century to the next.

Unlike other cities that appear to have grown

OPPOSITE AND ABOVE
The Institut du Monde Arabe (Institute of the Arab World) features a wall recalling the intricate latticework of Islamic art that has an unexpected practical purpose. Its 'artificial eyes' let in the sunlight. At night, the building's panoramic rooftop provides a perfect venue for trendy Parisian *soirées*.

organically, Paris has carved out its territory sporadically. It has responded to outside threats at different stages of its history by building ramparts and fortresses (traces of the foundations of the citadel – later to become the Louvre – engineered by Philippe-Auguste in about 1200, in order to keep *les Anglais* at bay, are still to be seen in the museum at basement level), and has modified its confines consistently at the onset of threatened or real invasions. From 1853 to 1870 Napoleon III's prefect, Baron Georges Haussmann, demolished medieval fortifications and replaced them with the tree-lined, neoclassical boulevards that are his signature.

One of the city's oldest and most famous monuments is Notre-Dame Cathedral, which dates from the twelfth century. An awe-inspiring symbol of religious magnificence, with its breathtaking rose window – at 10 metres (33 feet) wide, the largest on Earth, and unchanged in 800 years – it has entered popular culture through literature and films, not least the 1996 Disney adaptation of Victor Hugo's novel *Notre-Dame de Paris* (*The Hunchback of Notre Dame*, 1831). For children taken to the cathedral for the first time, clambering up to the roof through winding stairwells and getting a closer look at its monster-shaped gargoyles is a fabulous experience.

Some of the city's flagship edifices owe much of their presence to the fact that they were overtly intended as 'statesmen's statements' to posterity, most recently François Mitterrand's *grands projets*: Nouvel's Institut du Monde Arabe, I. M. Pei's Louvre pyramid, Dominique Perrault's Grande Bibliothèque (National Library) and the Grande Arche (Great Arch) at La

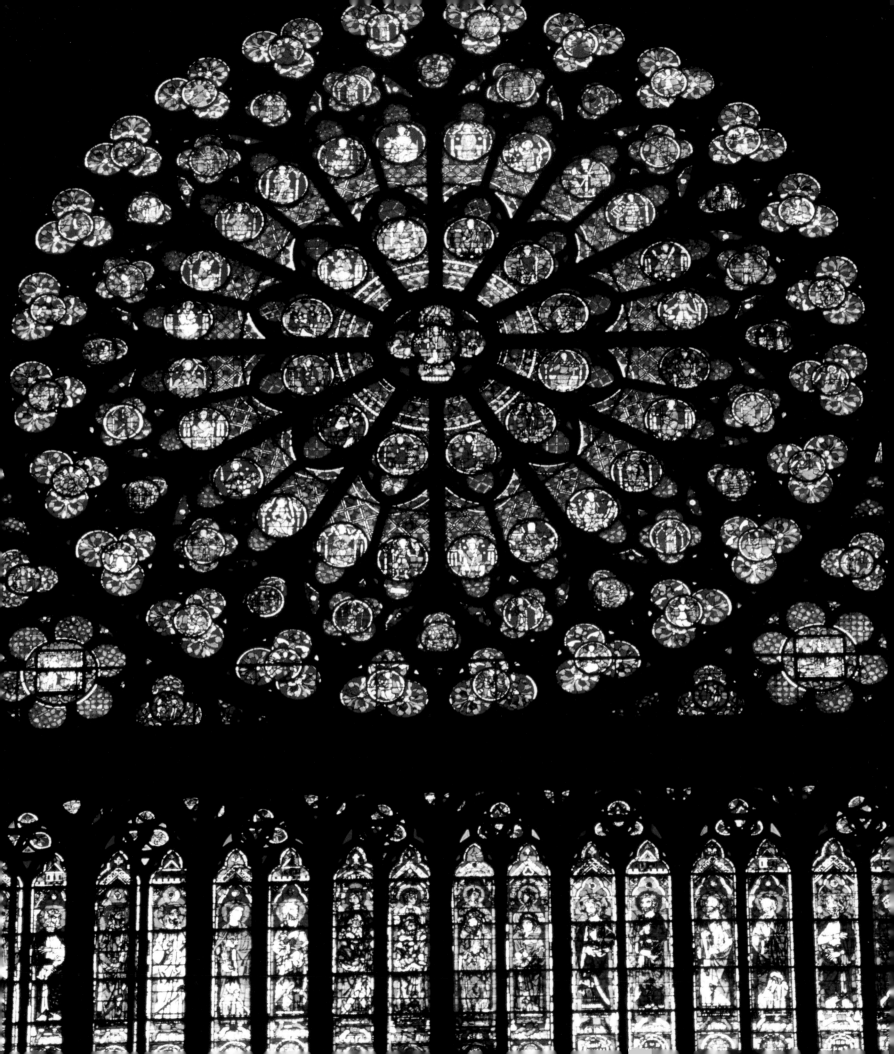

Défense, the business quarter. This was envisaged by the Danish architect Johan Otto von Spreckelsen as an 'arch of fraternity' that would prolong the perspective of Napoleon I's two previous triumphal arches – the Arc de Triomphe at the top of the Champs-Elysées, and its smaller Tuileries Gardens counterpart, the Arc de Triomphe du Carrousel. Nonetheless, other more intimate construction projects contribute to the cachet of the plane tree-lined avenues that are charac-teristic of Paris's *beaux quartiers* (beautiful districts).

In between periods of revolutionary upheaval and historic turmoil, the *grande bourgeoisie* left its imprint on the cityscape, bearing witness to its upper middle-class aspirations by erecting handsome private resi-dences known as *hôtels particuliers*. Today many of these stately mansions house museums that showcase prestigious collections of art and artefacts in an atmosphere akin to that of a private home.

ABOVE Already envisioned in the 1950s as a futuristic office and shopping complex, La Défense is famous for its Grande Arche. Conceived as a futuristic 'arch of fraternity', it was inaugurated in 1989 – just in time for the bicentenary of the French Revolution.

The Grande Arche of La Défense was envisaged as an 'arch of fraternity' that would prolong the perspective of Napoleon's two previous triumphal arches.

With its impressive façade – a replica of Marie-Antoinette's Petit Trianon at Versailles – the Musée Nissim de Camondo, near the Parc Monceau in northwest Paris, re-creates the domestic surroundings of an eighteenth-century dwelling, from grand salon to scullery. Filled with the finest Aubusson tapestries, furnishings, paintings and decorative objects, as well as rare Sèvres, Meissen and Chantilly porcelain, this rambling town house, built between 1911 and 1914, was bequeathed to the French state by Moïse Camondo in memory of his son Nissim, an aviator killed in combat in 1917. Born in Constantinople in 1860, Camondo

ABOVE A stately stairway leads up to the Nissim de Camondo Museum's sumptuous collection of eighteenth-century furniture and porcelain. **RIGHT** The Arc de Triomphe du Carrousel commemorates the military victories of Napoleon I. It is perfectly aligned with the much larger Arc de Triomphe crowning the Champs-Elysées, as well as the Grande Arche of La Défense.

The French Revolution

Heralded by the ideals of the Enlightenment philosophers, the French Revolution is a major political milestone. It abolished absolute monarchy in France and proclaimed a universal Declaration of the Rights of Man and of the Citizen on 26 August 1789 – just over a month after the storming of the Bastille.

On 14 July we celebrate Bastille Day, our national holiday, with a military parade on the Champs-Elysées that is regulated like clockwork. This can be confusing for tourists. In fact, the festivities last two days – beginning during the night of 13 July, when firework displays and *bals des sapeurs-pompiers* (popular parties hosted by local Fire Brigades) are scheduled throughout the city.

The rallying cry of the revolutionaries was *Liberté, égalité, fraternité, ou la mort!* (Freedom, equality, brotherhood, or death!). Now, a milder version of this motto – *Liberté, égalité, fraternité* – emblazons the façades of our capital's republican institutions. (Contrary to popular misconception, there is in fact no historical connection between the three words of the Revolution's tripartite slogan and our *tricolore* flag. Its three colours actually refer to a pre-revolutionary episode – a last-minute attempt to reconcile king and city: uniting 'royal white' and 'Parisian blue and red'.)

RIGHT An after-dinner stroll in the heart of historical Paris, along the canal that separates the Ile Saint-Louis from the Ile de la Cité, where the first stone of Notre-Dame was laid in 1163. The Cathedral's spire dominates the skyline.

belonged to a dynasty of enlightened bankers who were once described as 'the Rothschilds of the East'. Sadly, the museum's sumptuous atmosphere is imbued with further family tragedy: the discerning collector's only surviving child, Béatrice, was deported to Auschwitz concentration camp in 1944 with her husband and two children.

Undoubtedly, this and the other distinguished *hôtels particuliers* that have been transformed into delightful thematic museums possess a mysteriously engaging atmosphere, as though suffused with the family history of their long-gone occupants. Sometimes there was an ulterior motive behind their construction: the need to construct a paramour's love

nest, perhaps. The pretty Petit Hôtel Bourrienne at 58 rue d'Hauteville in the 10th arrondissement was home to flamboyant author and diplomat François Chateaubriand's petulant Creole mistress, Fortunée (a close friend of Joséphine de Beauharnais, the future Empress of France), before it was taken in hand by a sterner pair: Bonaparte's personal secretary Antoine Fauvelet de Bourrienne and spouse.

Musées insolites de Paris, a Parigramme guide that highlights unusual Parisian museums, describes the taste in decor of the de Bourrienne household as a permanent quest for symmetry, bordering on obsession: 'The motifs on the ceiling responding to the parquetry on the floor, the columns to the windows, the chandeliers to the rugs'. Such rigour was the antithesis of Fortunée's coquettish insouciance. Draped Grecian-style dresses were *à la mode* when she was the toast of the town, and she is reputed to have splashed water on hers before going out, in order to obtain the translucent effect so much in vogue in the late 1790s; she even went so far as to parade along the Champs-Elysées bare-breasted, claiming that underwear was unnecessary.

It is the sharp contrast between the liberated attitude of the artists, writers and other charismatic characters the city has always attracted and the strict, formal equilibrium of its architecture (for instance, the sobriety of its Haussmannian apartments, their lofty ceilings adorned with elaborate mouldings, and the topiary perfectionism of its gardens created by André Le Nôtre) that makes Paris a spectacular stage where anything can happen when you least expect it.

City of Light – or Lights?

Is Paris the Ville Lumière (City of Light) seen in the daytime, or is it the City of Lights seen at night, when illuminated monuments, neon club signs and seasonal lighting make it an essential tourist destination? Ignoring these clichés and stereotypes, which people invariably mention if they are asked to put the capital's indefinable magnetism into words, I ask why we should be made to choose between the singular and the plural. Why can't Paris be both 'City of Light' and 'City of Lights'?

In all fairness, the singular has many serious supporters. The American journalist David Downie uses it for his book *Paris, Paris – Journey into the City of Light*

(2005); it is also the version *Time* magazine opted for, choosing 'City of Light's Dark Side' as the headline for its review of Andrew Hussey's best-seller, *Paris: The Secret History* (2006), described as a 'biography' that 'depicts the capital as a seedy, violent town, yet still holds out hope for the future'.

'City of Light' is said to come from 'Paris – ville lumière', the slogan devised to promote the 1900 Exposition Universelle (World Fair) of international arts and technology, and its Palais de l'Electricité. In this dazzling pavilion the public was introduced to the diverse applications of electricity, which was presented as an innovative source of power and artificial light. All kinds of advances (for example, the possibility of television) were described in the inaugural speech, and film sequences by pioneering cinematographers Auguste and Louis Lumière were projected on to a screen. For the 1937 International Exhibition Raoul Dufy painted his world-famous *Fée électricité* (Spirit of Electricity) mural. A vibrant celebration of electrical energy and light, it was completed a year later, as the darker days of war and occupation approached.

However, Paris is also clearly a City of Lights, and in more senses than one. To nightbirds planning to do the rounds of the cabarets where the cancan was

OPPOSITE One of many posters by Henri de Toulouse-Lautrec spotlighting La Goulue, the Moulin Rouge dancer said to have created the French cancan.

born (starting with the Moulin Rouge), it conjures up glowing images of multi-coloured street signs and headlights flickering in the dark. (This is the capital that the dancer Josephine Baker took by storm in the 1920s, see page 143.) On the other hand, the pupils of prestigious Parisian *lycées* (grammar schools) bearing the names of eighteenth-century luminaries, such as Denis Diderot and Marie Jean Antoine Condorcet, are more likely to think of philosophical references in the context of 'Paris, ville des lumières'. Without a second's hesitation, those studying for the philosophy test – a crucial part of the baccalaureate exam that enables them to move up the educational ladder – will think of the Siècle des Lumières (Age of Enlightenment, a period during the eighteenth century when philosophers favoured reason and individualism rather than tradition).

Advocates of the plural form – City of Lights – maintain that Paris owes this sparkling sobriquet to a 'first': the installation of electric lights on the place de la Concorde at the end of the nineteenth century. What a historically charged square this is! Its Egyptian obelisk was presented to Charles X, King of France, in 1829 by Mehemet Ali, the Governor of Egypt, and was erected on its present site in 1833 during the reign of Louis-Philippe. Dating back to the time of the Egyptian pharaoh Rameses II, 13 centuries BC, it qualifies as the oldest monument in Paris.

Do bus conductors driving across this vast, traffic-clogged intersection during the rush hour think of it as the centre stage of bygone dramatic events? Probably not, and maybe it's just as well.

Created in 1748 in honour of Louis XV (le Bien Aimé, or Well-loved) to display an equestrian statue that was erected to celebrate his recovery from a life-threatening fever – and dismantled at the outset of the French Revolution in 1789 – this is the public square where the most infamous guillotine was set up. How daunting to stand in the middle of this bustling modern thoroughfare and think that crowds of vociferous Parisians once thronged to what was renamed the place de la Révolution to watch more than a thousand heads roll. Among them were the royals Louis XVI and his wife, Marie-Antoinette, and even some of the principal revolutionaries, including Georges Danton and Maximilien Robespierre, brought down by infighting and extremism respectively.

In the decades leading up to these events, proponents of the Enlightenment, whose ideas fuelled revolutionary thinking, cast another, intellectual, light on Paris society. People such as the philosopher Charles Montesquieu, the writers Pierre Marivaux and Pierre Beaumarchais, the economist Anne Robert Turgot, and the linguist Etienne Condillac met in the stimulating atmosphere of cultural salons hosted by 'enlightened spirits', women who had a knack for bringing sharp intellects together. These included Madame de Staël, Madame du Deffand and Julie de l'Espinasse. Brilliant minds, set on building a republic of letters, also discoursed chez Madame Geoffrin at her rue Saint-Honoré home.

Ironically, the address is within steps of a new millennium phenomenon. The Colette concept store is visited by fashionistas from all over the planet, seeking a more frivolous form of enlightenment: insights into the latest trends in high tech, arts and style. No ordinary boutique, it regularly exhibits the work of mainstream artists and photographers, and serves a huge selection of international mineral-water brands in its Bar à eau (Water Bar). In effect, it's the headquarters of fashion snobbism.

I'm told that Parisians tend to be viewed as intellectual snobs, that we are chic to the point of being intimidating, and that we frequently strike people as arrogant. Visitors complain about the surly waiter who gives them a dark look if they don't leave him an extra tip, even though service is included, or the unsmiling passenger sitting opposite them on the Métro, staring disapprovingly … at what? The clothes they're wearing? The book they're reading? Their shoes? Their hairstyle? I'm puzzled by these stereotypical visions of my fellow citizens, and hope we're not really like that.

Paris Landmarks

In his book *Paris, Paris – Journey into the City of Light*, David Downie describes *ville lumière* as 'a self-congratulatory catchphrase' still used today by Parisians to mean that the city is a 'spiritual and material beacon to the world'. It may seem pretentious to think of the place you live as a beacon, but I like the thought of Paris being a *ville phare* (lighthouse), and to me this is what the city is — a place that welcomes people in, rather than a supercilious capital bestowing its beauty and wisdom on the rest of the world.

When Parisians drive back to the city after the *grandes vacances*, the long, paid summer holidays that

ABOVE The Colette concept store (at 213 rue Saint-Honoré in the 1st arrondissement) has been the official headquarters of Paris fashion snobbery since it first opened its doors in 1997.
TOP The Bar à eau (Water Bar) at the Colette concept store serves a huge selection of international brands.

salaried workers have been entitled to since Léon Blum's Front Populaire government created them in 1936, they glance eagerly at the milestones and road signs indicating the distance that separates them from 'kilometre zero', the nationwide yardstick that tells hikers, bikers, lorry drivers and motorists anywhere in the 'hexagon' how far they are from Notre-Dame. To many of them, the prospect of returning to their homes conjures up images of a highly symbolic 'lighthouse': the Eiffel Tower. Controversial at the time it was built (for the Exposition Universelle of 1889), as newly unveiled monuments invariably are, this lofty, steel-girdered landmark conveys the atmosphere of Paris to travellers throughout the world, in the same way that the Statue of Liberty says New York even to somebody who has never been there.

As it happens, the Eiffel Tower and Statue of Liberty are related in more ways than one. In fact, they could be described as cousins. After all, it was Gustave Eiffel who designed the inner metallic framework of the Statue of Liberty, conceived by the French sculptor Auguste Bartholdi as a nod to the centenary celebrations commemorating America's independence. It took five years (from 1878 to 1882) to assemble this gigantic symbol of the spirit of liberty – dubbed *La*

Liberté éclairant le monde (Freedom Enlightening the World) – and during construction its scaffolding became a local curiosity in the Batignolles-Monceau district. Freshly annexed to the capital by Napoleon III and his architect–prefect Baron Haussmann as the 18th arrondissement, this part of Paris became a favourite destination for families promenading after lunch on Sunday afternoons. They all flocked to the rue de Chazelles to gaze at the draped, torch-bearing silhouette peaking out of the roof of the workshop where it was being decked with sheets of copper.

Does Paris have cause to be jealous of this American-sized symbol of one of its most cherished values – one that is integral to the revolutionary motto *Liberté, egalité, fraternité*, and that appears over the doorways of France's venerable republican institutions, from its free state schools (introduced by Jules Ferry in 1881) to its city halls, where mayors clad in tricolour sashes preside over civil-wedding ceremonies? Of course not. The Big Apple's statue has a little sister on the banks of the Seine, opposite the Maison de la Radio – General de Gaulle's large, rotund and very 1960s Broadcasting House *à la française*.

This smaller bronze replica of Bartholdi's Manhattan monument was practically a protagonist of Roman Polanski's espionage drama *Frantic* (1988), as it could be seen from a riverside barge that was crucial to the film's denouement. And it's no exaggeration to say that getting to see it up close is an adventure in itself. A stairway in the middle of the Pont de Grenelle leads to the Ile des Cygnes (Island of Swans), which has been the official home of Paris's mini Statue of

Liberty since its inauguration on 15 November 1889.

Donated to France in the name of the American expatriate community to mark the centennial of the French Revolution, it is meant to be looking at New York, presumably engaged in a bridge-building dialogue with its transatlantic sibling in accordance with the wishes of its creator. For reasons of protocol, however, this has not always been the case. It originally faced the Eiffel Tower so that it wouldn't turn its back on the Elysée presidential palace, but in the end Bartholdi won. As a result, it provides springtime honeymooners posing for souvenir snapshots with a superbly evocative backdrop. On a fine, cloudless day, they can capture two Parisian landmarks in a single picture: the Eiffel Tower and Liberty Jr.

Paris is full of other emblematic images that tell two or three stories at once. The most striking of these is the perspective of three of its triumphal arches. The place to head for is the Arc de Triomphe du Carrousel in the Tuileries Gardens. The trick is to photograph it in such a way that the obelisk on the place de la Concorde and the Arc de Triomphe on the place de l'Etoile, from which the capital's main avenues radiate, are aligned and therefore in focus simultaneously. Similarly, the pristine, streamlined Grande Arche at La Défense mirrors the latter, much photographed Champs-Elysées monument.

The first stone of the Arc de Triomphe was laid two centuries ago, on 15 August 1806 (the birthday of its originator, Napoleon Bonaparte), but its formal inauguration took place much later, on 15 December 1840, when Napoleon's ashes were returned to Paris after his death in exile on St Helena. The monument has witnessed an incredible array of triumphal

Immortalized in Movies

Since the Lumière brothers introduced cinematography to the City of Light, Paris has been the star and backdrop to countless films. Some perpetuate a romantic vision of the Paris Dream closer to *Amélie* than the *banlieues* (suburban) culture depicted in Mathieu Kassovitz's 1995 success *La Haine* (Hate).

A pioneer of French cinema, the 'ciné-magicien' Georges Méliès built one of the world's first film studios in his backyard at the turn of the last century, using trick photography to suggest Haussmannian architecture. However, he soon took his camera out on the boulevards, paving the way for future film-makers – including

Nouvelle Vague (New Wave) directors whose 'city movies' captured the mood of 1960s Paris.

Peppered with colourful sequences conveying Montmartre, the Opera and Notre-Dame among other Parisian locations, Vincente Minnelli's 1951 musical *An American in Paris* re-creates the bohemian surroundings of an artist living in a garret. Yet, as was the case for *Hôtel du Nord*, most of the street scenes in this MGM production, starring Gene Kelly, were shot on set.

The Métro is also a star. During the filming of cult 1970s thriller *Peur sur la ville* (Fear in Town), crowds applauded Jean-Paul Belmondo as he executed his open-air stunts, leaping from one carriage to another.

processions and solemn occasions, ranging from Napoleon III's flamboyant entry into Paris in 1852 to Victor Hugo's massively attended funeral in 1885; from the entry of German occupying forces during the Second World War to the collective joy unleashed when France was liberated; from the annual 14 July parade when aircraft perform tricolour victory rolls to the agony and the ecstasy of Tour de France cyclists speeding past the finish line. Within minutes of a Cup Final win, football fans yield to a massive euphoric impulse to invade the Champs-Elysées.

The vista from the Arc de Triomphe extends from the past glory and enduring prestige of the Louvre to the ambitions for the future symbolized by the Grande Arche, with its transparent tubular lift designed to propel aficionados of heady sensations to its roof-level gallery. As it rises, you'll see on the esplanade below – don't look down if you have a poor head for heights – hurried office workers and keen shoppers milling around La Défense, amid sculptures, murals and fountains commissioned from Joan Miró, Alexander Calder and other eminent artists. In the course of 2007 a space is to be opened in memory of Raymond Moretti, a sculptor and draughtsman who worked for many years in a studio based in this futuristic environment. Von Spreckelsen's 'arch of fraternity' looks on approvingly as jazz fans clap and tap their toes in time to jam sessions included in the programme of the Fête de la Musique, a free citywide music festival held on the first day of summer, 21 June, which was launched more than two decades ago by Jack Lang, François Mitterrand's flamboyant minister of culture.

Whether you look at the capital's landmarks from the Grande Arche, the Eiffel Tower or the top of its brand-new Musée du quai Branly, there is something unbeatably exhilarating about contemplating a panoramic view of Paris. Do not expect to be alone – others will also have responded to the instinct to survey the city from on high – but no matter. Don't let that deter you from enjoying this simple pleasure. Follow the example of Amélie, as played by Audrey Tautou in Jean-Pierre Jeunet's quintessentially Parisian film of the same name. In it she hides behind a telephone booth and beckons the fiancé of her dreams, Nino Quincampoix (Mathieu Kassovitz), to an ideal vantage point – namely, Montmartre's Sacré-Coeur – with a breathily whispered injunction: '*Monsieur Quincampoix, suivez les flèches et munissez-vous d'une pièce de 5 francs*' (Mr Quincampoix, follow the arrows and be sure to have a 5-franc coin). Like her, you know this is the type of childlike activity that makes life special; and zeroing in on the districts that combine to create the atmosphere of this beautifully laid-out metropolis is worth every penny you slip into the telescope.

OPPOSITE The Basilica of the Sacré-Coeur, seen from the 9th arrondissement. In the foreground is Notre-Dame-de-Lorette, the church where the Impressionist painter Claude Monet was christened. He was born in 1840 to second-generation Parisians who lived at 90 rue Lafitte (to the right of this view).

Conservationists accustomed to describing the white dome of Sacré-Coeur in detail, or curators keen to impart their knowledge of the Louvre's little-known masterpieces, may not approve entirely, but the success of *Amélie* (aka *Le Fabuleux destin d'Amélie Poulain*, 2001) and the later *The Da Vinci Code* (2006) have exerted a considerable influence on the behavioural patterns of sightseers planning a visit to Paris. Thematic guided tours that take their cue from both are in tremendous demand, and the impact is such that 'Amélie Poulainization' of Montmartre has been observed, causing property prices to soar. Tourists throng to the film's principal locations: the Café des Deux Moulins (15 rue Lepic) and Au Marché de la Butte (56 rue des Trois Frères), a corner shop that has become a chic *épicerie fine* (delicatessen), proudly emblazoned with the sign it sported in *Amélie*: 'Maison Collignon, fondée en 1957'.

Across the city, on the Left Bank of the Seine, is Montparnasse, once the hub of Parisian artistic life. It was frequented by the writers Paul Verlaine and Oscar Wilde during the nineteenth century, before its offbeat – now smart and renowned – café-restaurants (La Closerie des Lilas, La Coupole, Le Dôme, La

ABOVE LEFT
Abbesses, the Métro stop for
Montmartre. The area has
undergone an 'Amélie
Poulainization', following the
box-office success of Jean-
Pierre Jeunet's whimsical film
comedy, *Amélie*, which starred
Audrey Tautou. **ABOVE RIGHT**
Au Marché de la Butte (56 rue
des Trois Frères), the corner
shop in the movie.

Rotonde, Le Sélect) became the preferred haunts of
later ground-breaking artists, poets and authors
(Pablo Picasso, Max Jacob, Amedeo Modigliani,
Chaim Soutine, William Faulkner, Man Ray), who met
there from the 1920s onwards, essentially to keep
warm and exchange creative viewpoints over coffee or
cheap wine.

In case you're wondering why Montparnasse is so
called, it gets its name from a huge pile of rubble that
once stood where the crossroads of boulevard du
Montparnasse and boulevard Raspail now stands.
Seventeenth-century university students ironically

nicknamed it 'Mont Parnasse', the French name for Mount Parnassus, the heavenly residence of ancient mythology's muses.

At present, Montparnasse is dominated by a towering 56-storey skyscraper, the Tour Montparnasse, whose coin-operated telescopes offer a 360-degree panorama that allows the curious to peer at the tombs of deceased celebrities, such as Charles Baudelaire, Guy de Maupassant and Serge Gainsbourg, who are interred in the nearby Père-Lachaise cemetery. In sharp contrast to the impersonality and modernity of the Tour Montparnasse is a nearby cobblestoned alleyway housing traditional artists' studios. This is also the home of the Musée du Montparnasse, which stages thematic shows that re-create the atmosphere of this arty territory's heyday. In a courtyard at the very end of this picturesque alleyway the museum has installed an atelier/exhibition space, unveiled in 2003, that pays homage to the Franco-Brazilian environmentalist/artist Frans Krajcberg.

While Montparnasse is associated with the artists of the early twentieth century, the Pompidou Centre – widely known as Beaubourg (see page 169) – is the showcase for those of today. Co-designed by the Anglo-Italian team of Richard Rogers and Enzo Piano, when it first hit the headlines in 1977 it was suspected of being a *machine à fabriquer des statistiques* (a machine destined to produce favourable attendance figures). Sceptics asserted that visitors would race up its intestine-like escalators merely to ingest the extraordinary view of Paris, as opposed to doing so for the sheer delight of attending events connected with

RIGHT Spring in the Père-Lachaise cemetery, where such poetic spirits as Frédéric Chopin, Oscar Wilde and Edith Piaf are interred.

contemporary art; the result, they argued, would be that these turnstile-tippers would be erroneously counted as consumers of cultural products. Naturally, this was long before modern marketing methods revolutionized the public's attitude to culture. At the Pompidou Centre, as elsewhere, it has become advisable to book by telephone or via the Internet when planning to visit multi-sponsored blockbuster exhibitions. It is true that the view from Beaubourg's gastronomic restaurant, the Georges – named as an allusion to Georges Pompidou, the president behind the project – is exceptional, but in the space of three decades the centre has contradicted its detractors: this multi-disciplinary museum has proved that twentieth- and twenty-first-century art can attract uninitiated members of the general public who come for more than the view.

The Paris Dream

Which of these two mental images most epitomizes Paris? A sepia-tinted postcard of the city from a *bouquiniste* (a stall by the Seine where you can buy second-hand books and posters), or the electronic response on a mobile telephone to a GPS-guided search of the *Michelin Guide*? The answer is that neither image is totally representative. This legendary city is constantly reinventing itself as it endeavours to encompass its rich and eventful past, its current question marks and the prospect of an exciting if uncertain future.

At the beginning of the twenty-first century a new wave of multi-disciplinary designers has decided to adopt an approach to the urban environment that crosses the boundaries between different specializations. Among these is Matali Crasset, whose mentor was Philippe Starck, the well-known designer who fitted out Eurostar's Business Class lounge at the Gare du Nord. Crasset co-runs Lieu commun, a shop dreamt up in association with friends with whom she shares common ground: Ron Orb, who designs ergonomic clothes, and the disc jockey Laurent Garnier, a founder of the FCommunications French Touch record label. In 2005 Crasset showed MIXtree, a set of armchairs equipped with interactive digital musical controls, in 'D.Day – le design aujourd'hui' (Design Today), a forward-looking exhibition presented at the Pompidou Centre.

Promoted as the Capital of Style or Creation, Paris has a reputation for being inspirational. France's answer to the American Dream, the Paris Dream continues to impel students with a penchant for the arts to cross the Atlantic and seek a *chambre de bonne* (a myth in itself, since there is no longer such a thing as an inexpensive 'maid's room') where they will paint the ultimate masterpiece or write the definitive novel. The dream goes back to the 'Lost Generation', a description applied to a group of illustrious expats that included Ernest Hemingway, Ezra Pound and F. Scott Fitzgerald (see pages 160–1). The term was coined by Gertrude Stein, the Paris-based author and art collector, to describe a generation of poetic spirits marooned in the city of enlightenment in the wake of the First World War.

ABOVE A bird's-eye view of the Pompidou Centre, which was opened in 1977 and named after its initiator, President Georges Pompidou.

The Pompidou Centre has proved that twentieth- and twenty-first-century art can attract uninitiated members of the general public, who come for more than the view.

The Paris Mosaic

How do I visualize my city? Perhaps as a mosaic of atmospheres asserting their distinctive identities within the constraints of elegant avenues, ancient ramparts and freshly defined boundaries planned with the precision of a military battle. *Paris je t'aime* (Paris I Love You), a global co-production that opened the *'Un Certain Regard'* category at the 2006 Cannes Film Festival, reflects this aspect of the capital. While its title harks back to the lyrics of a popular tune sung by Maurice Chevalier, it sets out to update a certain rose-tinted vision of Parisian life, presenting a fresh view of the City of Light, or Lights.

A kaleidoscopic homage to Paris, which is shown as an excellent setting for a love story (be it a romantic interlude, intense parental rapport or just friendship), *Paris je t'aime* enlisted the talents of 18 leading film-makers, relying on a multiplicity of genres and scenarios to translate the atmosphere of the city's distinct neighbourhoods. What makes this unabashedly sentimental film so interesting to anyone attempting to see Parisian life 'through the looking glass' or 'beyond the keyhole' is that each director was asked to encapsulate a particular district or arrondissement in a five-minute segment.

In charge of the 1st arrondissement, the Cohen brothers chose to depict a disorientated tourist (Steve Buscemi) waiting for a train at the Tuileries Métro station. As we find out later (because *Mona Lisa* postcards fall out of the paper bags he's carrying), this innocent bystander, who becomes involved in a French lovers' quarrel because he happens to be in the wrong place at the wrong time, had just been to the Louvre. The outcome of this cautionary tale of two cultures is the reverse of Hollywood's predictable happy endings.

Each of the cinematic vignettes is served by a small cast of actors (Nick Nolte, Juliette Binoche, Gena Rowlands, Willem Dafoe, Natalie Portman) whose characters reveal a particular facet of Paris's present personality through a series of culture shocks and human rapprochements. On its release some commentators used the phrase 'new melting pot' to describe what the film portrayed, but I prefer my mosaic metaphor — the perception of this capital as an atmospheric mixture of multi-cultural influences that retain their identity while being part of a bigger picture.

In Alexander Payne's 14th arrondissement contribution the director follows the solitary peregrinations of an unaccompanied American traveller (Margo Martindale). At the beginning of the film the camera observes her staring out of the window of a comfortable, albeit impersonal, hotel room. Throughout the segment she recounts the circumstances of her visit to Paris in faltering French. Her tone of voice is curiously touching. We soon realize that she's reading from an essay she has been assigned to write for an adult-education class. Finally, she has a smile on her face. Sitting on a bench in a children's playground, she tells us that her trip has taught her a great lesson. What she loves about Paris is that the city has made her 'feel alive'.

All Parisians have their *madeleines de Proust*, those things that trigger memories of perfect days spent with someone special — days that made them, too, feel alive – in the same way that the madeleine dipped in tea reminded Marcel Proust of youthful encounters, as he recalled in *À la recherche du temps perdu* (In Search of Lost Time, 1913–27). Gourmands will fondly recall meals enjoyed in Paris restaurants that have kept the elaborate nineteenth-century panelling and brass fittings prevalent in Proust's time. In the rue Montorgueil, to which Queen Elizabeth II went during a state visit that coincided with the centenary of the Entente Cordiale (the understanding reached between Britain and France in 1904), the specialist snail restaurant L'Escargot d'Or boasts a painted ceiling that was once in Sarah Bernhardt's residence, and Le Rocher de Cancale greets its faithful customers with a rock-shaped, oyster-embossed, cast-iron sign that attests to its expertise in seafood.

Paris and its unforgettable atmosphere! The city may come across to newcomers as 'clean cut, like a French mind'; as being excessively attached to its inner and outer limits, strapped in not only by its ring road, but also by its *petite ceinture* (little belt) bus service, which links what were once the gates in the city's walls – its inhabitants constricted by centuries of conformity to codes of conduct, as thrifty home-makers obliged to tighten their belts can be. But, come what may, frivolity is never far off in this urban mosaic with its distinctive districts whose residents are instantly distinguishable – though this is less true than it was – from one quarter to the next: from popular east to residential west, from commercial north to bohemian south, from well-turned-out Right Bank to more unconventional Left Bank.

Vive la différence! On the ultramodern, conductorless Meteor Métro line that whisks its passengers from the place de la Madeleine to the Bibliothèque Nationale (National Library) in a matter of minutes, stylish Parisians can be transported from one place or atmosphere to another – from tea and macaroons chez Ladurée after a shopping spree in the rue du Faubourg Saint-Honoré's luxury boutiques to an exhibition paying tribute to a major graphic artist – at what feels like the speed of light.

ABOVE Marlon Brando sweeps co-star Maria Schneider off her feet in Bernardo Bertolucci's 1972 film *Last Tango in Paris*, which was set in the city.

Every station in the Métro public-transport system tells a story, from Passy in the heart of the distinctly snooty 16th arrondissement (its stairway seen in *Last Tango in Paris*, 1972) to *banlieue* destinations, such as Saint-Denis Stade de France, the stop for the football stadium that was built for the 1998 World Cup. Although each station is unique, they are unified by their Art Nouveau entrances, which make the system a Parisian icon in its own right – a star of our city.

One final word of advice: appearances can be deceptive. As the sociological and cultural critic Walter Benjamin put it, however rigorously planned a beautiful capital such as Paris may be, it only seems to be homogeneous. In reality, our city is a *mélange* of hidden surprises and unexpected delights. Who would guess that the venerable Café de la Paix could be 'cool'

when they walk past its crowded terrace? Yet it serves fluffy 500-feuilles (half-sized millefeuilles) 'signed' by fashion designers, such as Agatha Ruiz de la Prada, Agnès b. and Paco Rabane.

Le fun and what is fashionable are not where you expect them to be. Admittedly, most of Paris's world-renowned hotels – notably the Crillon and the Plaza Athénée with jet setters' limousines parked permanently in front of revolving doors besieged by hordes of groupies in search of celebrity autographs – are in the 8th arrondissement's glamorous *triangle d'or* (golden triangle). Nevertheless, alternatives to these swanky establishments are springing up in unexpected quarters all over town. In the Marais there is the Hôtel du Petit Moulin, whose decor by Christian Lacroix features brightly patterned, retro-futuristic

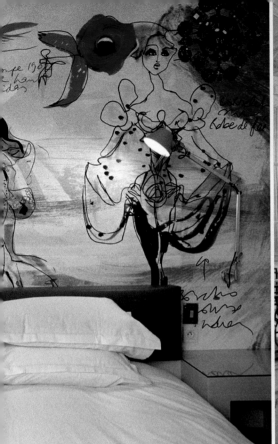

ABOVE LEFT Jet setters' sports cars parked outside the Plaza Athénée on the avenue Montaigne, which is famed for its high-fashion boutiques, from Chanel to Dior.

ABOVE CENTRE An alternative to *palace* hotels like the Plaza, the Hôtel du Petit Moulin in the Marais was decorated by star fashion designer Christian Lacroix.

ABOVE RIGHT The majestic corridors of the Crillon, familiar to the guests of this renowned place de la Concorde *palace*.

furnishings that resemble his couture line, and Thierry Costes chose the 9th arrondissement for the Hôtel Amour – a wink at the love nests associated with this district.

So here you have my Paris – a picture-perfect city of contradictions (the glories of the Age of Enlightenment versus the horrors of the French Revolution) and contrasts (medieval Notre-Dame versus the late twentieth-century Pompidou Centre), of magic and mystery. It is only possible to scratch the surface of what makes Paris unique, but in the chapters that follow I will take you through centuries of Parisian panache and turmoil to reveal some of the history – ancient and modern – that lies behind this ever changing and atmospheric City of Light. Let the show begin …

CITY OF LIGHT, CITY OF DARKNESS

It may be tempting to forget the capital's darkest hours and think of it instead as the source of eighteenth-century Enlightenment, particularly when ambling along the banks of the Seine on a sunny day.

The grandiose names given to two of France's star centuries – the seventeenth, dubbed the Grand Siècle (Great Century), and the eighteenth, known as the Siècle des lumières (Age of Enlightenment) – are intended to symbolize the military and cultural glory of their mainly Versailles-based monarchs. However, there was a dark side to the dazzling image of the second era. The pomp and splendour of court life existed alongside poverty and hardship among the populace as a whole, and the disparity fomented discontent that led, some would say inevitably, to the French Revolution (see page 28).

It may be tempting to forget the capital's darkest hours and violent historical episodes, and think of it instead as a City of Light, as the source of eighteenth-century Enlightenment and nineteenth-century innovations, such as photography and cinema, particularly when ambling along the banks of the Seine on a sunny day. From the Ile Saint-Louis, a haven of tranquillity with its seventeenth-century buildings, to the Grand Palais of 1900 with its stunning, newly restored glass-and-metal roof, the city's distinctive forms of architecture are positively breathtaking, even to long-standing Parisians. Yet such beauty is the fruit of bitter struggles as well as grand visions; and the narrow alleyways nestled behind imperious boulevards and elegant squares harbour dark secrets.

Like the quintessential 'ice queens', such as Grace Kelly, who featured in Alfred Hitchcock's films noirs, Paris's blond-stone monuments, its mighty mansions, Gothic masterpieces and elegant statues seem impervious to the dramatic events they have witnessed. Most daunting of all, the infamous Conciergerie prison boasts a roll-call of illustrious inmates, ranging from Maximilien Robespierre to Marie-Antoinette, while shadowy streets a stone's throw from Notre-Dame were privy to a legendary medieval romance.

The grand passion of Abelard and Héloïse ranks with that of Shakespeare's Romeo and Juliet. Abelard, a scholar and priest, had a passionate affair with Héloïse, who was less than half his age. Her uncle,

Fulbert, both Abelard's landlord and his boss (he was the canon of Notre-Dame's school of religion and philosophy, where this brilliant thinker was pursuing his studies), had asked his lodger to be his bright young niece's tutor. So far, so good. However, so great was the passion that Abelard felt towards his pupil that he married her in secret and she became pregnant. Furious, Fulbert had the culprit hunted down and emasculated.

This gruesome denouement didn't prevent the estranged lovers exchanging ardent letters, which have continued to fascinate major literary figures over the centuries, among them Geoffrey Chaucer and Alexander Pope. Indeed, Pope's poem 'Eloisa to Abelard' supplied the title of Michel Gondry's 2004 film *Eternal Sunshine of the Spotless Mind*. Although Abelard and Héloïse are rarely evoked these days, their cult reached its climax in the nineteenth century, when the ill-starred couple's remains were transferred to the Père-Lachaise cemetery, and their love nest (9 quai aux Fleurs, near the Hôtel de Ville) was rebuilt.

The story of the lovers is recounted in detail in Andrew Hussey's gruesomely well-researched *Paris: The Secret History* (2006), which is filled with lurid accounts of our capital's direst episodes, starting with the grisly execution of François Ravaillac, the religious fanatic who assassinated Henry IV. While this book perhaps fills the need for an alternative guide to the city, I'm a little concerned that many readers may remember only its gruesome passages, focusing on sex, dirt and violence, as if our city hadn't suffered enough from such clichés.

Certainly, though, the tug of war between passion and reason – the pivotal contradictions that define Jean Racine's and Pierre Corneille's Grand Siècle tragedies – is always somewhere around the corner, like a call to order. And nowhere are those contradictions better examined than in the plays from the classical repertoire staged at the Comédie-Française, which I watched as a student, perched up in the theatre's *poulailler* (gods).

The Français, as our national theatre is frequently called, has come a long way since 1680, when its figurehead, Molière – it is sometimes called La Maison de Molière – first staged his comedies in and around the Palais Royal before a *parterre* (pit) of riotous hecklers overlooked by supercilious courtiers in comfortable seats. This celebrated actor, dramatist and theatre director didn't die on stage, as is often asserted, but at home, ironically after collapsing during a performance of *Le Malade imaginaire* (The Hypochondriac). In this satirical play he lampoons those whose obsession with their health makes them prey to quacks and charlatans. Today 40 rue de Richelieu, the site of the lodgings where this protégé of Louis XIV drew his last breath, accommodates an avant-garde art gallery (Galerie Artcore).

The Comédie-Française itself is like a living museum, with hundreds of paintings and sculptures displayed throughout the theatre, alongside memorabilia connected with the time-honoured company's most prestigious actors or pensionnaires – items such as Molière's watch and the creaky old wheelchair used in *Le Malade imaginaire*. In 1996 the American film-maker Frederick Wiseman made a documentary capturing every aspect of daily life at the Français, from gala evenings to backstage organization and box-office trivia.

Undoubtedly, the theatre possesses a special atmosphere that continues to motivate contemporary creative spirits. On the fashion front, leading couturier Christian Lacroix designed the costumes for a recent Comédie-Française production of *Cyrano de Bergerac*. Written by the late nineteenth-century neo-Romantic poet and dramatist Edmond Rostand, the play has inspired a variety of modern reinterpretations, with international stars in the title role. These include Placido Domingo (at New York's Metropolitan Opera), Christopher Plummer (in a Broadway musical), Gérard Depardieu (in a French screen version) and Steve Martin (in the Hollywood film *Roxanne*).

Lacroix told me that one of his many sources of inspiration was Rose Bertin, an 'Ab Fab' eighteenth-century dressmaker, who relied on surprisingly modern marketing methods to promote her designs with 'panache' – a word that's said to have entered the English language via a translation of *Cyrano*. Like modern designers, Bertin presented a fresh collection for each change of season. Her muse was the queen, Marie-Antoinette, whom court painters portrayed wearing her creations, much as current style-setters are featured on the cover of *Vogue* sporting haute-couture trends. Bertin's signature accessory was whimsical *poufs* – decorative details, such as flowers, fruit and feathers, that were threaded into the wearer's hair or wig. They usually had a seasonal or topical twist – for

instance, a serpent to mark Louis XV's smallpox inoculation, or a balloon to celebrate the world's first manned flight, by the Montgolfier brothers, in 1783.

Mise en Seine

Much of Paris's irresistible magnetism rests upon the magic rapport between the River Seine and the city's splendid riverside architecture reflected in its waters. On the *quais* or quays that run along its embankment the quality of the light is unique, both by day and

night. Could there be a downside to such a seductive river? Perhaps a narcissistic undercurrent reminiscent of the words of the malevolent queen in Charles Perrault's 1697 fairy tale *The Sleeping Beauty*: 'Mirror, mirror on the wall, who is the fairest of them all?'

From Honoré de Balzac to Charles Baudelaire, prominent literary figures have described the Seine as a dark ocean tinged with violence and passion. Guillaume Apollinaire's romantic poem 'Pont Mirabeau' stresses its melancholic aspect:

Passent les jours et passent les semaines
Ni temps passé
Ni les amours reviennent
Sous le Pont Mirabeau coule la Seine.

(Days pass, weeks pass
Neither past time
Nor past loves return
Under the Mirabeau Bridge flows the Seine.)

ABOVE Dawn on the canal running between the Ile Saint-Louis and the Ile de la Cité – in the presence of two key Parisian landmarks: Notre-Dame Cathedral and the Pantheon. In January 2007 President Chirac unveiled a plaque in this neoclassical mausoleum that houses the graves of France's eminent historical figures. Dedicated to unsung heroes recognized as 'Righteous' by Israel's Yad Vashem memorial, its inscription pays tribute to ordinary citizens who saved the lives of Jews during the Second World War.

Downside or not, in the beginning was the river. Its banks were the site of the settlement established by the Parisii, the Celtic tribe to whom Paris owes its name, before the Roman invasion in the first century BC. Even these earliest Parisians were torn between adopting a rational approach to the Seine (making the most of the advantages it offered for their principal daily activities of farming and trading) and fearing the disastrous consequences of living alongside it (flooding and disease). Although practical – they exchanged

coins and relied on maps to return to their huts after hunting expeditions – these hardy quarrymen lived in awe of the river, and attributed magical powers to its waters.

The history of Paris as a real town with a street plan, and wooden bridges linking it to the Seine's islands (one in the vicinity of today's Pont au Change, near the Hôtel de Ville, another near the Petit Pont in the 5th arrondissement), begins in 54 BC, when Julius Caesar conquered the Parisii's settlement, which he called Lutetia. By the first century AD, the Romans had shifted the city centre to the slopes of the Montagne Sainte-Geneviève. Officially named 'Paris' (*Civitas Parisiorum*) two centuries later, the freshly proclaimed capital of Gaul withdrew to the Ile de la Cité when it came under threat from Germanic assailants.

Richly illustrated old textbooks are proudly displayed on the second-hand bookstalls opposite Notre-Dame that remain one of the Seine's great tourist attractions. Their volumes emphasize the civilizing influence of the Roman Empire on 'our Gaulish ancestors', telling us that our forebears learnt to wash in hot

OPPOSITE *Bouquinistes* (open-air booksellers) first appeared on the banks of the Seine – during the construction of the Pont-Neuf bridge – at the turn of the sixteenth century. They continue to attract both tourists and book-loving Parisians.

ABOVE Vineyards in the city. This bucolic setting is not quite as anachronistic as it looks. Today, Montmartre's annual *vendange* (grape harvest) perpetuates Paris's winemaking tradition, which dates back to the Roman times.

and cold thermal baths built on sites that still exist (at the Musée de Cluny and the Collège de France). The Romans converted the local population to their way of life, adding a forum and strictly aligned cemeteries to their haphazard riverside agglomeration.

The Gauls were soon taking the axiom 'When in Rome …' a step further. They started to behave more like Romans than the Romans themselves, mimicking their speech, attire and classical architecture – an attitude summed up in an expression coined in the nineteenth century: '*Etre plus royaliste que le roi*' (To be

more royalist than the king). Molière's *Le Bourgeois gentilhomme* took lessons in how to become a gentleman, with fatal consequences familiar to theatre lovers all over the world. In the end, he was neither himself (a jovial entrepreneur) nor acceptable to the disdainful aristocrats whose lifestyle he sought to emulate. The moral of the story? To succeed, just be yourself.

The Romans also introduced vineyards on the Left Bank, keeping their wine in huge, two-handled vessels called *amphorae*, and serving it in saucer-sized dishes that were passed around from one guest to another – a form of *art de vivre* that was heartily encouraged by the fourth-century emperor Julian. Today, the Montmartre *vendange* (grape harvest) is an annual celebration that perpetuates Paris's wine-making tradition and dates back to those times. Sold

in aid of local charities, the Clos Montmartre is one of our capital's sole-surviving urban vintages, a vestige of the 18th arrondissement's wine-producing past, which is reflected in the names of several of the area's quarters, including the Goutte d'Or (Golden Drop).

For centuries the Seine continued to define the shape of the city, with the Ile de la Cité, in the middle of the river, its civic heart – the headquarters of its political and religious leaders. This is where Paris's first Christian sovereign, the Frankish king Clovis, established his court in 506. The city was declared the capital of France in 987, and over the years the Right Bank became its trading arm. Goods were unloaded at the place de la Grève, where the Hôtel de Ville, or town hall, now stands. On the other hand, the Left Bank was the city's *éminence grise* (power behind the throne), the area where churches and universities gained

St Bartholomew's Day Massacre

It was 1572, a dark year for religious reformists in France, when, wittingly or not, Catherine de' Medici sparked one of the most dreadful massacres in the country's history. The Reformation advocated by Martin Luther and John Calvin had won many converts to Protestantism, creating a climate of conflict that in 1562 culminated in the Wars of Religion between Catholics and Huguenots (French Protestants). In what should have resulted in an alliance between both sides, the queen-regent had arranged a marriage between her daughter, Marguerite of Valois, and the Protestant Henry of Navarre. The month set for the wedding was August.

Before dawn on 24 August – St Bartholomew's Day – the bells of Saint-Germain-l'Auxerrois (the old parish of the kings of France, within steps of the Louvre) rang for the morning prayers and that is when the slaughter started. In the capital alone, several thousand Protestants – notably guests in town for the royal wedding – were killed, the doors of their lodgings having been marked with a cross. Four centuries later, in 1972, a street (rue de l'Amiral de Coligny) was named after their leader, Gaspard de Coligny, who was murdered in gruesome circumstances – possibly at the instigation of Catherine de' Medici.

LEFT Notre-Dame after dusk. The Cathedral's façade exudes a magical aura that fascinated the Symbolist and Surrealist writers of the late nineteenth and early twentieth century.

ground in the Middle Ages. As a matter of fact, there's an old saying that incorrigible cultural snobs continue to reiterate: '*La Rive Droite dépense, la Rive Gauche pense*' – The Right Bank spends while the Left Bank thinks.

Notre-Dame Cathedral stands on the island itself. It has been said that this medieval symbol of spiritual and regal supremacy rests on the Seine's waters 'like a great and majestic ship'. Completed in the second half of the thirteenth century, its construction changed the status of Paris, turning the city into a pilgrimage centre with an appropriate cathedral – by far the tallest building it had ever known. Until the sixteenth century it was the scene of the annual Fête des Fous (Festival of Fools), when its priests and their congregations took part in a bawdy pagan ritual that officially permitted them to let their hair down for a day.

Fascinating to the Symbolist and Surrealist authors of the late nineteenth and early twentieth century, Notre-Dame is the setting for great literary classics peopled by strange protagonists, such as Victor Hugo's hunchback and Rabelais' Gargantua. These mysteriously compelling characters permeate the cathedral's towers, just as the monster-faced gargoyles perched around the crenulated roof are part of the very fabric of the building. We know they are only waterspouts with a practical purpose, but, like ramshackle scarecrows, they make us feel slightly uneasy.

Architecture and Boundaries

Over the centuries, French architects have pursued an intermittent love affair with classicism, sporadically breaking away from its formal constraints to create more whimsical styles (from the rock and shell motifs in vogue under Louis XV to Art Nouveau), but constantly reconquered by its obvious elegance and inbuilt sense of history. Harking back to the distant past, their taste for rigorously aligned façades and columns may well have deep-seated roots in the Roman occupation of Gaul. Boosted by the rediscovery and excavation of Pompeii, classicism reached unprecedented heights when Baron Haussmann transformed Paris into a neoclassical incarnation of Napoleon III's imperial dream.

Classicism or romanticism? Reason or passion? Are the frontiers between these opposites as clear cut as they appear to be? The year 2006 marked the bicentenary of the death of Claude Nicolas Ledoux, the architect of the wall of the Farmers-General customs

ABOVE Arch after arch, column after column, the Louvre palace deploys the beauty of its time-honoured architecture, in perfect harmony with Pei's pyramid, as the sun rises.

It was francis 1 who decided to restore the capital's medieval fortress and transform it into a palace in the style of the Renaissance.

barrier/toll-gate system put up around Paris under Louis XVI to levy taxes and attempt to limit the city's size. Looking at Ledoux's principal architectural legacy, the Saline Royale saltworks at Arc-et-Senans in the Doubs region near the Swiss border, it is impossible to dismiss this utopian visionary as a mere mathematician set on building cupolas and colonnades. Like his contemporary fellow architect Etienne-Louis Boullée, he had a non-classical approach to classicism.

These maverick architects, both esteemed as pillars of neoclassicism, pushed the limits of their genre. They even experimented with *architecture parlante* (talking architecture), imagining buildings and statues whose shapes were determined by their purpose: a hoop-maker's cottage just like a barrel, and a brothel in the shape of a gigantic phallus.

Paradoxically, Ledoux's work came to be seen as typical of the *ancien régime* (the old order before 1789), and his formidable barrier of Farmers General tollgates was demolished during the Revolution. Parisians had felt imprisoned by the wall, a 24-kilometre (15-mile) stone barrier that corresponded roughly to what are now routes 2 and 6 of the Métro , and felt it provided cover for shady characters and generated crime and disease. What remains of Ledoux's ambitious enterprise? A token number of what were once his toll-

gates, such as the La Villette rotunda on what is now the place de Stalingrad, and the Barrière du Trône on the place de la Nation, have definitely maintained an air of authority.

The demolition of the Farmers General is a striking example of how Paris differs from other French cities. Many of them are former garrison towns surrounded by ramparts, and it is logical that they should convey an impression of timeless impregnability. Our capital is more like a patchwork of enclaves with imperceptible limits, and each arrondissement is composed of distinct quarters. Parisians notice changes of atmosphere as they circulate from one part of the capital to another, but are not always aware of the historical reasons for these sudden variations. Some of the streets or boulevards they hurry along every day follow the contours of historical fortifications that were later torn down.

In *L'Invention de Paris* (The Invention of Paris, 2004) Eric Hazan elucidates the way the city has developed from one century to the next, gradually growing into the fresh boundaries its consecutive rulers and governments have 'invented' in order to confront specific economic or political challenges. He uses two simple metaphors to describe this evolution, one scientific and the other linked to nature. He sees

An Effervescent Court

There have been vineyards in the Champagne region since the Gallo-Roman period, but the appellation *vins de Champagne* wasn't introduced until the seventeenth century, when Henry IV served these pleasant, but as yet non-sparkling, wines at court. It has often been suggested that a Benedictine monk, Dom Pierre Perignon, an exact contemporary of Louis XIV, invented champagne, but this is not the case. However, he can be credited with developing a number of techniques that helped to elevate the *méthode champenoise* to a fine art.

Champagne became *de rigueur* at the court of Louis XV, and was much enjoyed by his most celebrated mistress, Madame de

Pompadour, whom he promoted to marquise in 1745. She is supposed to have declared that it is the only wine to leave women looking beautiful after they've drunk it. Marie-Antoinette is also part of the champagne legend: the shape of the round glasses from which this sparkling wine is traditionally drunk is said to have been moulded on her breast – the 'saucy' source of inspiration of an artist whom the Sèvres Porcelain Manufactory had commissioned to design a set of saucers especially for the queen's dairy at the château de Rambouillet!

ABOVE LEFT Marie-Antoinette, in an eighteenth-century painting of the French school, wearing decorative hairpieces known as *poufs*, which were the height of fashion at the time.

ABOVE François Boucher's portrait of Madame de Pompadour reading a book, most probably by one of her Enlightenment protégés.

Paris's transformations as a centrifugal progression reminiscent of the concentric rings in a tree trunk. Even when they're located at opposite ends of the capital, quarters that were built simultaneously have an *air de famille* (family resemblance).

This is the case with upmarket Passy and lively, multi-ethnic Belleville in the 20th arrondissement, on the capital's northeastern periphery. Historically a working-class area, home in 1871 to the strongest supporters of the Paris Commune (a revolutionary government set up by republicans), Belleville has preserved eye-catching architectural treasures. The Pavillon de l'Hermitage (148 rue de Bagnolet) is an example of the rambling mansions built by the late eighteenth-century bourgeoisie. Only slightly less remarkable than the handsome *hôtels particuliers* favoured by the upper-crust Parisians of Passy (see page 24), these buildings were called *pavilions*, a term now applied to *pavillons de banlieue* — more modest, late twentieth-century family houses that are characteristic of the city's leafy suburbs.

ABOVE Place de la Bastille. Since the opening of Paris's new Opéra-Bastille inaugurated on the 200th anniversary of the storming of the Bastille (13 July 1989), this area has become a hub of Parisian nightlife. Its lofty column was built to commemorate the Trois Glorieuses (three 'glorious days') that heralded the downfall of Charles X in July 1830.

Hazan also describes how the city's resistance to attackers has contributed to its development. It was saved by St Geneviève, after whom the Montagne Sainte-Geneviève is named, when it was attacked by the Huns in 451. Then it was taken over by the Franks in the sixth century, and set on fire by the Normans in 857. It was saved once again by Count Eudes, an ancestor of the Capetians, the dynasty that ruled France from the tenth to the fourteenth century. Paris had no intention of remaining passive in the face of its enemies. From early times its territory-conscious warriors constructed rudimentary fortresses and ramparts to ward off assailants, redefining boundaries in the process. Hazan has a theory about the effects of this strategy on how the city grew, and he's found a name for it: the 'psycho-geography of the limit'.

Convinced that no other Western capital has developed in quite the same way as Paris, he explains that the pattern has always been the same. Throughout history, every time its leaders decided to re-centre the city or modify its limits they allowed for only a little extra space or leeway between the previous agglomeration's inhabitants and the reassessed confines (walls or toll-gates). Sooner or later the population overflowed, and living conditions became intolerable. In the interests of trade and security, it became necessary to replan the town and reappraise its frontiers.

From Philippe-Auguste's fortress and city-encircling walls, envisaged to keep the Plantagenets out two decades before construction was completed (around 1200), to the Périphérique (ring road) that allows motorists to circumvent the city centre and marks the frontier beyond which taxi fares increase, France's capital has reinvented its limits on half a dozen occasions. Nothing is left of the stone 'curtain' added to Philippe-Auguste's fortifications in the fourteenth century by Charles V, who beefed them up and also erected the Bastille, itself dismantled in 1789 at the outset of the French Revolution, its stones sold off as souvenirs, just as pieces of the Berlin Wall were sold two centuries later. Hordes of angry revolutionaries

had broken into this dreaded dungeon, only to discover a handful of relatively harmless inmates: four counterfeiters, a couple of madmen and a startled young gentleman. The prison was no longer the instrument of oppression they had assumed it to be. Nonetheless, its storming is recalled as the spark that ignited the Revolution, and to this day 14 July is celebrated as marking one of the great turning points in human history. It's said that rules are made to be broken. Perhaps that's why, one after the other, Paris's walls have been reduced to rubble.

Of course, walls can turn against their masters. During uprisings insurgents have been known to use them against the governments they were intended to defend. When this is the case, those in power have them removed with as much zeal as they were built. Louis XIV ordered the demolition of the medieval ramparts that had done the monarchy such a disservice at the time of the Fronde, a two-part anti-royalist

OPPOSITE The Louvre viewed from the Left Bank of the Seine. Students of the Ecole nationale supérieure des Beaux-Arts (the National School of Fine Art) walk across the Pont du Carrousel or (more bohemian) Pont des Arts to study the museum's great masterpieces.

revolt that lasted from 1648 to 1653, and was led first by the nobility and later by urban commoners. His childhood memory of the rebellion haunted him and was responsible for his adult apprehensions about living in Paris. Tree-lined boulevards replaced Philippe-Auguste and Charles V's venerable fortifications, which didn't prevent Louis yielding to the vanity of triumphal arches commemorating his victories: the Porte Saint-Denis and Porte Saint-Martin are his oeuvres.

Then there are the so-called *enceinte de Thiers*

fortifications initiated three decades before the Paris Commune of 1871 by Adolphe Thiers, the French statesman who repressed this revolutionary movement. Demolished in the 1920s, they followed the circular outline formed by the *boulevards des maréchaux* (broad streets named after Napoleonic generals) that are the starting point of Paris's latest T3 tramway system. In a peculiar historical turnabout, our capital's ancient borders have been recycled as thoroughfares that permit its citizens to circulate freely from one city gate to the next.

Seat of Power

Since the seventeenth century Versailles has epitomized the glories of Louis XIV's reign and been a universal symbol of regal splendour, but the seat of power in France has more often been in Paris. To begin with, from the tenth century to the early part of the fourteenth, the country's rulers were based on the Ile de la Cité. And the Palais de la Cité – later the Conciergerie, a fearful prison during the French Revolution, and now part of the Palais de Justice law courts – was the historic seat of government. Eminently chilling even

now, its three towers rise above the waters of the Seine like ghosts from another age. The Tour d'Argent (silver tower) housed the royal treasures; the Tour de César (Caesar's tower) evokes the Roman occupation; the Tour Bonbec ('Good Beak' Tower) is notorious for its torture chamber. Also intact since the Middle Ages, the Salle des Gens-d'Armes (Hall of the Men at Arms), with its vaulted ceiling and lofty columns, is a gem of Gothic architecture; it's hard to believe that this magnificent room was just a staff canteen that fed around 2000 royal employees a day. Medieval kings must have required a vast retinue to keep them safe … Indeed, it was Philippe-Auguste who introduced the first police force (still known as *gendarmes*) to Paris in an attempt to bring some order to its dark and unruly streets.

By the mid-fourteenth century not even the Palais de la Cité was deemed secure enough for city-based monarchs, who were afraid of both the local population and threats from external enemies. Future kings would live in a yet more impregnable fortress on the Right Bank: the Louvre. First built by Philippe-Auguste in about 1200, it was added to by Charles V in the fourteenth century. In the centuries that followed – its construction spanned 600 years – Francis I, Catherine de' Medici, Henry IV, Louis XIII, Louis XIV and Napoleon would also leave their mark on the palace.

It was Francis I who, set on transferring the royal household from the Loire Valley to Paris, decided to restore the capital's medieval fortress – in a state of ruin since the reign of Charles V, which had been marked by the Hundred Years War with England – and transform it into a palace in the style of the Renaissance. The king was a leading proponent of the movement, which had originated in fourteenth-century Italy and was popular in France from the fifteenth to the early seventeenth century, and a patron of Leonardo da Vinci. His top acquisition? 'The most famous painting in the most famous museum in the world.' Kept behind bullet-proof glass, the *Mona Lisa* or *La Gioconda* has been the object of countless wild theories designed to reveal its secrets – if secrets there are. The least that can be said is that it has been over-exposed; but, above all, it remains a very beautiful portrait. Da Vinci spent his whole life trying to improve the likeness, and the result is nothing short of extraordinary. It comes alive to the extent that it doesn't even look like a painting. It is more like real flesh on real bones.

Francis I's great legacy to the Louvre was the Salle des Caryatides, the most astonishing large-scale Renaissance interior in Paris. Constructed by Pierre Lescot, it is named after the four caryatids (female-shaped columns) sculpted by Jean Goujon to support the hall's music rostrum. Regrettably, the patron–king didn't live to see the final result as he died in 1547, three years before it was inaugurated. By then, only the southwestern section was finished. Work on the Louvre continued under Henry II and Charles IX, and two more wings were completed within about thirty years.

In 1564 one of French history's most mystifying figures came on the scene and built the Tuileries Palace, which would later be linked to the Louvre.

OPPOSITE The Parisian dream lives on in the capital's leafy enclaves. Even apparently formal settings, such the Luxembourg gardens (on the Left Bank) or the Tuileries, possess secret havens of tranquillity. (The main Tuileries garden was originally conceived by Catherine de' Medici in the ornate Italian style, before being re-designed in the French manner by the noted seventeenth-century landscape gardener, André Le Nôtre.)

OVERLEAF Shaped like a monumental king crab, the Louvre faces the historical centre of Paris. The museum's present-day visitors can enter and leave the building via the Tuileries Gardens.

After Henry II's death his widow, Catherine de' Medici, broke with the long-established tradition of wearing loose, white robes while in mourning; instead, she dressed only in black, and instructed the ladies of the court to don tightly corseted gowns. This strict attire must have accentuated her stern countenance as she supervised the progress of her cherished project. Lauded by her fans as a brilliant patron of the arts, this powerful and controversial Florentine was accused of the worst ills by her detractors, who saw her as a Machiavellian wheeler-dealer who was exploiting France's divisions for her own aggrandisement. Visitors to the château de Blois in the Loire Valley can see the cabinets where the poisons she's alleged to have used against enemies were kept.

Philibert de l'Orme, the architect to whom she assigned the construction of the Tuileries Palace, claimed that Catherine de' Medici showed a real interest in how the building developed. Erected on a piece of land adjoining the Louvre that had belonged to *tuiliers* (tile manufacturers) – hence its name – it featured a garden that she designed herself in the Italian style, dotting it with fountains, grottoes and mazes.

Long overshadowed by her spouse's favourite, Diane de Poitiers (whom she sent into exile after his death), Catherine was Regent of France from 1560 to 1563, during the minority of Charles IX, the second of her three sons, who acceded to throne after the death of his brother Francis II. Like other rulers and leaders before and after her, Catherine de' Medici was anxious about what lay ahead. Her good-luck charm was a kabbalistic medallion, and she consulted Nostradamus, the French physician and astrologist, and his Florentine counterpart, Cosimo Ruggieri. They predicted her future and she listened. When Ruggieri told her she would die in the palace's parish, she left the Tuileries for a *hôtel particulier*, erected where Paris's impressively domed nineteenth-century Bourse du Commerce (produce exchange) stands today.

All that remains of the building is the much visited Ruggieri Column, which dates back to 1572. Decked with the intertwined initials of Catherine and Henry, its purpose is shrouded in mystery. Did the Italian astrologer use it to study the stars? Who knows. What is certain is that Ruggieri relied on an assortment of dubious rituals, including sticking pins into dolls that represented his enemies, a kind of Renaissance voodoo.

Catherine de' Medici is interred with Henry II in the Basilica of Saint-Denis, the resting place of the kings of France, in a two-tier sarcophagus, a bit like a bunk bed for the dead. At the top of this *memento mori* a sculpture represents the deceased at prayer, while the bottom part is much more disquieting. Evoking an allegory of life and death, it depicts the corpses, complete with worms and shrouds. The tomb is a marvel of Renaissance statuary, adorned with carvings exuberantly executed by the mannerist sculptor Germain Pilon.

Entering the basilica is an unsettling experience. Guidebooks describe it as France's royal necropolis, and, along with other places of worship, Saint-Denis was ransacked and desecrated during the French Revolution. It was reinstated when the monarchy was restored in 1814. The following year remains assumed to be those of Louis XVI and Marie-Antoinette were removed from the churchyard of the Madeleine and reburied in the basilica, given pride of place in a special chapel. Francis I, Henry III and Louis XV are all said to be buried here. The hearts of the Sun King and his father, Louis XIII, are kept in small caskets, along with a 'piece' of Henry IV. And in 2003 the mummified heart of the dauphin – the boy who would have reigned as Louis XVII – was sealed in the wall of its crypt. Whether you are a royalist or not, this is an affecting memorial.

The next monarch to take charge of the Louvre was Henry IV who, as Henry of Navarre, had been the son-in-law in the marriage scenario envisioned by Catherine de' Medeci. After his accession to the throne in 1589, he forged ahead with a *grand dessein* (grand design) for the palace. Assisted by the Duke of Sully, his chief minister, he embarked on a sixteenth-century developer's project. Sweeping aside almost all the Louvre's medieval vestiges, he masterminded the construction of a *cour carrée* (square courtyard) to link the Louvre and Tuileries palaces. Parisians living in the area between them were not necessarily pleased at the prospect of their properties being expropriated, but the alteration to the site was oddly modern. Mezzanine apartments and ground-floor shops were built, a concept not far removed from the commercial concourse in the Carrousel du Louvre, next to I. M. Pei's glass pyramid, a *grand projet* of France's twentieth-century president, François Mitterrand.

Politically, Henry IV had a dream. Reconciliation was his strategy, even if the odds were against him. As a Protestant leader, he had besieged the capital, but in the interests of peace he had abjured his reformist convictions, affirming that 'Paris is well worth a Mass', and from then on had done everything in his power to become popular. First and foremost, he fed the citizens of the city, which earned him the sobriquet 'king of the *poule au pot*', a kind of chicken casserole. And his upgrading of the capital's oldest bridge, the Pont-Neuf, was perceived as a symbol of renewal. The Eiffel Tower of its time, it linked Left Bank and Right Bank, Ile de la Cité and the Louvre. (Three centuries later, in 1985, Christo – the French artist known for wrapping up anything from monuments to mountains all over the world – gave this bridge his special treatment, and thus brought it a new wave of admirers.)

Despite his efforts towards reconciliation, in 1610 Henry IV was assassinated for religious reasons, and it was the turn of his son, Louis XIII, to put his mark on the Louvre. The king was faced with the need to restore a building that functioned somewhat like the embassy districts of certain capitals today: viewed from the outside, it gave the impression of being a single autonomous diplomatic estate, but inside it was more like an ambassadorial village. Each ambassador had a residence, with a separate entrance and garden. Believing that all this had to change in favour of greater unity, Louis called on Catherine de' Medici's and Cardinal Richelieu's architect–engineer *protégé* Jacques Lemercier, who built the Palais Royal at the latter's request, to modernize the Louvre. Unfortunately, he died before he could bring this ongoing family project to fruition, and Nicolas Poussin left Paris for Rome without completing the murals the king had commissioned from him.

The Grand Siècle

On his deathbed in 1715 Louis XIV asked to be absolved because he had enjoyed waging war too much. What about the arts? How did this unabashed absolute monarch, a firm believer in the divine right of kings, do on that front? In this domain, as in other enterprises, the Sun King – so named because he brandished a sun-shaped symbol when he paraded on horseback at a festival held in the Caroussel du Louvre to celebrate the birth of his son – adopted a combative attitude from the early years of his reign. He regarded architecture as a priority, and founded a school that became a hotbed of talent. In addition, concerned about his soldiers' welfare, he commissioned the architect Libéral Bruant to design a hospital for military invalids (Les Invalides, graced with a domed chapel by François Mansart). He also assigned Bruant to convert Louis XIII's Salpêtrière arsenal into a workhouse–orphanage, which was later reconverted into a modern university hospital, whose neurosurgical unit was in the headlines after Princess Diana's fatal accident.

Louis XIV became king in 1643, at the age of five – the start of a long reign spanned by the overt grandeur of the Grand Siècle – and until 1651 Anne of Austria, Louis XIII's widow, was Regent of France. Although there was a considerable Italian influence on the court during this period – her adviser, Cardinal Mazarin, to whom she delegated full power, was born in Italy – the

RIGHT Louis XVI and Marie-Antoinette with their family at Versailles on 6 October 1789, as depicted by the Hungarian-born painter Gyula Benczúr (1844–1920). On that day a mob of angry Parisians, mostly women, had stormed the palace. The painting shows the monarch and his clearly distraught retinue clustered together as revolutionaries mill around the royal apartments.

Louvre was hardly modified. But as of 1660, and by royal ordinance of Louis XIV, the grand design begun by Henry IV was relaunched and placed in the hands of the Sun King's head architect, Louis Le Vau. Remembered as a virtuoso of the French Style, Le Vau injected his classicism with a particular brand of baroque lyricism, seen to greatest effect in the façade of Vaux-le-Vicomte, a château he conceived in collaboration with his habitual Versailles team (the painter–decorator Le Brun and the landscape gardener Le Nôtre). He decorated the king's bedroom in the Louvre and embellished the Tuileries Palace, once again in association with Le Nôtre, who replaced Catherine de' Medici's Italianate park with a formal *jardin à la française* (French-style garden). In tandem with Le Brun, Le Vau rebuilt the Louvre's Galerie d'Apollon, which had been destroyed by fire in 1661. This constituted a major architectural statement, a blueprint for the king's brilliant 'A-team', who were about to take charge of an infinitely grander project that would threaten Paris's leadership as the stylistic capital of France: the Palace of Versailles. Continually re-embellished until the mid-nineteenth century, the gallery is dominated by a central vault showing Apollo slaying a python, painted by Eugène Delacroix in 1851.

From 1665 to 1680 Claude Perrault, brother of Charles Perrault, the modernist author best remembered for his retelling of children's stories such as *Cinderella*, oversaw the construction of the Corinthian colonnade flanking the Louvre's east wing. Not merely an architect, but also an anatomist (among the founding members of the Academy of Sciences),

he translated a ten-volume manual written by the pioneering Roman architect–engineer Vitruvius into French, and so contributed to the dissemination of classicism throughout Europe.

The Sun King had summoned the Italian sculptor and architect Lorenzo Bernini, known for his monumental masterpieces and baroquely expressive carvings, such as his *Vision of St Theresa* altarpiece in Rome's Santa Maria della Vittoria church, but Perrault's relatively rational design was chosen over and above the Italian's more adventurous proposals. While in Paris, Bernini produced a number of sculptures representing illustrious figures; in particular, his bust of Louis XIV set the style for future royal portraits.

Louis XIV's minister of finance, Jean Baptiste Colbert, envisaged the Louvre as a symbol of the Sun King's cultural influence and economic clout – a glowing emblem of Colbertism (defined in business-school manuals as a form of protectionist, export-driven mercantilism, according to which a state's power and grandeur are ensured by the abundance of money circulating within it). Colbert's determination to keep the cash flowing inside the country had a strong impact on the kingdom's arts and style scene. A pioneer of the *exception culturelle* (the privileged status the French state is said to attribute to culture), he backed all manner of design projects, declaring that, 'Fashion is to France what the gold mines of Peru are to Spain'. Workshops employing the best craftsmen within the kingdom and beyond established standards of excellence designed to discourage imports and boost the sovereign's image abroad.

The Reign of Terror

Mere mention of the word Terror with a capital 'T' evokes visions of executions and severed heads brandished on stakes. The statistics are grim. By all accounts, the Revolution claimed the lives of tens of thousands of French citizens. At least 16,000 were guillotined, not all of them aristocrats. Indeed, more than half of them were peasants or labourers and about a quarter belonged to the bourgeoisie.

To be precise, there were two successive waves of Terror. The first lasted just over a month, beginning in the wake Louis XVI's destitution, before being cut short by the proclamation of the Republic in September 1792. A special tribunal hounded

suspected enemies of the Revolution, but the mob deemed it too slack with the Royalists, which led to a spate of random executions that went down in history as the September Massacres.

Known as the *Grande Terreur* (Great Terror), the best-known Reign of Terror started on 2 June 1793 when the Legislative Assembly's Girondist members were arrested *en masse*, accused of conspiring with the English to restore the monarchy. Ironically, it came to a halt with the execution of its chief instigator, Robespierre, who was guillotined without trial on 27 July 1794.

Initially spearheaded by Henry IV, the Gobelins tapestry and upholstery factory on the Left Bank of the Seine was purchased by Colbert on behalf of the king. Under the royal painter Le Brun, who lived on the spot, all kinds of furniture and jewellery were produced in its well-equipped premises, but the scope of its multi-disciplinary activities had to be reduced. As a consequence of the king's extravagant military campaigns, the establishment was closed in 1694, and reopened three years later as a tapestry workshop, which supplied mainly the royal household.

Work was suspended during the French Revolution and under Napoleon Bonaparte, but resumed with the Restoration of 1814. In 1826 the Savonnerie (a former royal carpet factory) was merged with Gobelins to create a state-run institution, which partly burnt down during the Paris Commune of 1871. Expert in the selection of dyes and the execution of tapestries so finely woven that they could be mistaken for paintings, the workshops have preserved an international reputation on a par with that of the Sèvres Porcelain Manufactory.

Fear and Loathing in Paris

Revolution was in the air, and the monarchy's dread of the capital and its citizens had its roots in events that had arisen in the seventeenth century. Although a child too young to govern at the time of the Fronde, an uprising in which insurgents fought with *frondes* (catapults), Louis XIV was nonetheless affected by it. This rebellion was not only the reason why he had Paris's medieval fortifications destroyed; it was also the motive behind one of his first kingly decisions: not to make the Louvre his palace. On coming of age, Louis resolved to transform a simple hunting lodge built by his father, Louis XIII, into a showcase for his kingdom's absolute supremacy in the domains of politics, fashion and the arts. Versailles was born.

Nevertheless, during the eighteenth century — a flamboyant if bloody era — the royal household had been established in the capital. In 1715, within weeks of the death of the Sun King, Philippe II, Duke of Orléans, picked the Palais Royal opposite the Louvre as the seat of power. Acting as regent before the young Louis XV's accession to the throne, this ex-war hero, who is most remembered, somewhat unfairly, for his much caricatured propensity to debauchery and gluttony, turned the royal palace into an open court. The general public could mill around its arcades, joining in a non-stop, pleasure-seeking saraband, and even watch operas almost free of charge. At first the duke was popular, notably for publishing essays previously censored by Louis XIV. However, the corrupt climate of his regency, which was notorious for supporting the aristocracy, infuriated local parliamentarians, who thronged regularly to the palace entrance and threw stones at his coach.

By 1722 the duke was left with no alternative but to relocate to Versailles, which became the backdrop to Louis XV's extramarital romances. The king treated Madame de Pompadour to a handsome Parisian town house that would become today's Elysée presidential palace. Yet for the next few decades the monarchy itself steered clear of the city, fearing parliamentary

ABOVE Known as the place de la Concorde since the end of the Great Terror, the place de la Révolution was the scene of over a thousand executions, including those of Louis XVI on 21 January 1793 and Marie-Antoinette later that year. The guillotine was transferred to the place du Trône-Renversé (Toppled Throne Square), on the site of today's place de la Nation, before being brought back to the place de la Révolution especially for the execution of the Terror's chief instigator, Maximilien de Robespierre.

unrest and human contact with its rough and rowdy populace.

Was it wise for the royal family to cut itself off from the population? Perhaps not. However, as it turns out, its apprehensions were justified. At the height of the French Revolution Paris was the setting for a spiral of irreversible events that sealed the fate of Louis XVI and his wife and children. When Versailles was stormed in October 1789, both Louis and the National Assembly were obliged to move to the capital, and from then on things got steadily worse. The king and Marie-Antoinette were placed under house arrest in their new home, the Tuileries Palace. In 1791 their request to spend Easter in leafy Saint-Cloud was rejected, and in the summer their attempted flight from Paris failed when they were intercepted at Varennes and forced to return to the capital.

The royal couple's Parisian misfortunes were accelerated by the storming of the Tuileries in August 1792, after which they were moved to the Temple prison, an ancient fortress built by the Knights Templar under the Ile Saint-Louis. Louis XVI was executed on the future place de la Concorde (known then as the place de la Révolution and previously as the place Louis XV) on 21 January 1793, and in October Marie-Antoinette was transferred to a bleak Gothic cell at the Conciergerie before she was guillotined. Throughout her trial she was addressed as Veuve Capet (Widow Capet), an ironic allusion to the Capetian dynasty from which her husband traced his descent, and was subsequently decapitated by the people of Paris. Two years later, at the age of ten, the dauphin, the heir apparent, who was instantly designated Louis XVII by unflinching royalists, died of tuberculosis in the prison where he had been held with his father, mother and sister.

Thousands of ordinary citizens also died, both in the September 1792 massacres, when inmates of Paris's prisons, suspected of being involved in counter-revolutionary plots, were beheaded, and in the course of the Second Terror (1793–4) drummed up by Jacobin leader Maximilien Robespierre's *régime*

RIGHT The place de la Concorde as it is today, visited by smiling tourists who pose for holiday snapshots in front of its famous obelisk. In the foreground, one of two fountains designed by the German-born architect Jacques-Ignace Hittorff (at the suggestion of Louis-Philippe, 'King of the French' from 1830 to 1848) add a note of serenity to this historically charged spot.

ABOVE Le Baron Rouge, one of Paris's last old-style wine bars, next to the Marché d'Aligre food market in the Bastille district.

d'exception. The place de la Concorde is the execution site with which Parisians are most familiar, but (as discussed later) there were other squares where the population had been accustomed to gathering when convicted criminals were put to death.

The Revolutionary Legacy

Anyone who wanders through the capital's oldest quarters, in the manner of the nineteenth-century boulevardiers that Edmund White describes in his aptly subtitled *The Flâneur: A Stroll through the*

Paradoxes of Paris (2001), will sooner or later come upon eerily vivid vestiges of the French Revolution and its aftermath. Right next to the Voltaire Métro station (named after the Enlightenment's most outspoken writer, essayist and philosopher) a plaque indicates the spot where the local guillotine was installed after several paving stones had been removed to accommodate it. On the rue de la Roquette or passage de la Main d'Or a few isolated artisans' workshops struggle to maintain their eighteenth-century identity in the bustling Bastille district, overtaken by chain stores, cafés and restaurants. And passing through a *porte cochère* (carriage porch) on the rue du Faubourg Saint-Antoine may reveal one of the sole remaining pockets of Parisian village life – a mews-style courtyard, where the cobblestones have remained unchanged since a certain 14 July when the carpenters and cabinet-makers of this craftsmen's quarter stormed the Bastille. The outline of the site where the prison used to stand is marked on the ground in front of the Café Français.

How can so much have survived those turbulent times? Altogether, fourteen churches were burnt to the ground in a spate of anti-religious ardour that swept through the city amid the Reign of Terror. Happily, neither Saint-Julien-le-Pauvre, said to be Paris's oldest church, nor Louis IX's Sainte-Chapelle were included. The demolition of Notre-Dame was decreed, but fortunately the cathedral survived, though it was briefly demoted. Along with a number of Parisian churches, it was temporarily divested of its sacred status. All its bells, apart from its *gros bourdon*

(the largest and deepest-sounding), were melted down, and the cathedral was successively converted into a storehouse and a stable. As for the statues on its façade, they were treated to a collective guillotine-like decapitation because they were thought to be effigies of the kings of France. As it happens, they represented the kings of Judah. The originals were ultimately unearthed in the cathedral's cellar in the mid-1970s, but by then it was too late to make amends: they had already been replaced.

Educational institutions, such as the Sorbonne, and several places of prayer were saved by the fact that they were temporarily 'recycled' as glorified warehouses. The antiquary Alexandre Lenoir retrieved religious works of art confiscated by revolutionaries in order to create a collection that would be the basis of a museum dedicated to French monuments.

The Picpus cemetery (at 35 rue Picpus) is an important destination for anyone embarking on a grand tour of revolutionary Paris. As burial grounds go, it is as sought after as an exclusive club. It is the capital's sole private cemetery, and word has got around that only the descendants of upper-crust victims of the Revolution can be put on its waiting list. Within walking distance of the place du Trône or place du Trône-Renversé (Toppled Throne), now the place de la Nation, where over fifty people were guillotined every day at the height of the Second Terror, the garden witnessed mass burials. The decapitated bodies of shopkeepers, soldiers, labourers and innkeepers were flung into communal graves alongside those of members of the clergy and nobility. Among those subjected

helped her to buy the rest, and a proper cemetery was created next to the mass graves.

The US flag flies over one of the tombs at the Picpus cemetery, a seemingly incongruous sight, for which there is an excellent explanation. Even though he wasn't guillotined, Marie Joseph Lafayette, who fought alongside the colonists in the American War of Independence, is buried here – next to his wife, whose mother and sister were beheaded and thrown into a communal grave.

Countless guillotined Parisians ended up in the Catacombs, which were constructed in disused, Roman-era limestone quarries shortly before the Revolution. The aim had been to find extra space for the corpses overcrowding the city's graveyards, especially the Cemetery of the Innocents in the centre of Paris, the stench that had been a local source of complaint for months. Things came to a horrific head in 1780, when cellars on the rue de la Lingerie collapsed under the weight of thousands of corpses, causing even greater distress to local residents.

'Arrête! C'est ici l'Empire de la Mort!' exclaims an inscription at the entrance to the Catacombs' neatly laid out ossuary, advising visitors to keep out of death's empire. A senior civil servant who had been in charge of the quarries had had a flash of inspiration: why not brighten up this underground mausoleum by piling up the bones in meticulously sorted categories? Thigh bones with thigh bones, shin bones with shin bones and skulls with skulls.

The Revolution's relentless upsurges of terror brought wave after wave of corpses in need of

to this bleak fate were sixteen Carmelite nuns, subsequently beatified in 1906.

This 12th-arrondissement burial ground is situated on land seized from the convent of the Chanoinesses de Saint-Augustin during the course of the Revolution, and is currently administered by the Sisters of the Sacred Heart. The story goes that in 1797 an aristocratic lady, whose brother was interred in one of the pits, secretly acquired some of the land. Approximately five years later, friends and family

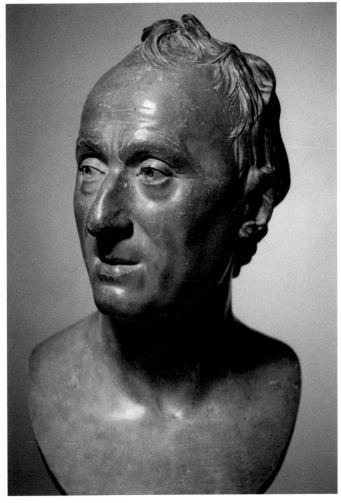

accommodation. Among the six million anonymous Parisians united in this democratic if macabre underground cemetery is a distinguished group of historical figures, ranging from Age of Enlightenment luminaries to high-ranking revolutionaries: Jean Paul Marat, assassinated in his bath; Georges Danton, guillotined with his long-time associate Camille Desmoulins, who was catapulted to celebrity on 12 July 1789 when he leapt on to a table outside one of the cafés in the Palais Royal, calling the public to arms; last but not least,

Maximilien Robespierre, 'the Incorruptible', who was beheaded in July 1794. Some would say there was an element of poetic justice in the downfall of this agent of the Reign of Terror – one of the last victims of the very regime whose decrees he had enforced with unprecedented intransigence.

The year 1789 is a milestone for many reasons, not least the start of the French Revolution and the election of George Washington as the first President of the United States. It also marks the foundation of Paris's National Assembly (parliament) and its Declaration of the Rights of Man and of the Citizen in preparation for France's first constitution, approved two years later. Asserting that we are 'born – and remain – free and equal' and that everyone is to be guaranteed the 'rights of liberty, property and freedom to resist oppression', its principles echo the precepts developed some seventeen years earlier by the Age of Enlightenment thinker Jean-Jacques Rousseau in his *Du contrat social* (Social Contract), which established the liberties and qualities that define a free subject.

The famous German Enlightenment philosopher Immanuel Kant was profoundly moved when told about the storming of the Bastille, aware that it marked a historical turning point. The Revolution stood for the freedom of spirit that he had always upheld. And as the next century's events would confirm, this was neither the first nor the last time that the population of former Gaulish Lutetia would opt for insurrection, preferring this uncertain political path, paved with bloodstained cobblestones, to social and political deadlock.

RIGHT *Liberty Leading the People.* Delacroix's best-known painting ranks high among the Louvre's great attractions. Even if the *tricolore* flag at the centre of the composition is generally associated with the spirit of the French Revolution, it's worth bearing in mind that it was completed in 1830, a year marked by the three-day 'July Revolution' known as the Trois Glorieuses. Deemed too inflammatory by the governments of that troubled period, it wasn't put on public display until after the Revolution of 1848, by permission of the Second Republic's freshly elected leader, Napoleon III.

Madame de Sévigné's house in
the Marais district is a
Renaissance jewel transformed
into a museum par excellence.

Lightness and Dark

From 1677 to 1696 Madame de Sévigné, an outstanding woman of letters, resided in a *hôtel particulier* (the Hôtel de Carnavalet) in the heart of the Marais district, at 23 rue de Sévigné. Her thirty-year correspondence with her daughter provides impressionistic insights into the subtleties of daily life in the seventeenth century, while the house itself is a Renaissance jewel transformed since then into a museum par excellence.

The Musée Carnavalet is the place to visit to get a grasp of the city's history – *in situ* – and to see the events of the seventeenth and eighteenth centuries in the context of the capital's development. The museum occupies two adjoining mansions, and its extensive collection is presented in panelled rooms with period furnishings. The main section, housed in the Hôtel de Carnavalet, Madame de Sévigné's original residence, documents the history of Paris from prehistoric times to the eighteenth century, while the Hôtel le Peletier de Saint-Fargeau mansion, which dates back to the seventeenth century, provides complementary insights, with displays of historical objets d'art and modern-day artefacts. Technically speaking, the buildings are not direct neighbours. They are separated by a school – the Lycée Victor Hugo – and linked by a first-floor gallery.

Inspired by the Château of Ecouen, Madame de Sévigné's *hôtel particulier*, built around courtyards with a garden in the middle, served as a model for other town houses, and boasts masterly sculptures by Jean Goujon. It was bought by the City of Paris in the mid-nineteenth century at the suggestion of Baron

ABOVE LEFT Among the Marais district's Renaissance gems, Paris's vast Musée Carnavalet is not only devoted to the history of the capital, but also organizes exhibitions focusing on living artists and photographers.

ABOVE RIGHT A portrait of Madame de Sévigné by Claude Lefebvre. Remembered for the witty and colourful correspondence she addressed to her daughter, Madame de Sévigné moved into the Hôtel de Carnavalet in 1677.

Haussmann, and houses a number of architectural elements salvaged from historical edifices that were destroyed to fulfil the streamlined vision of Napoleon III's town-planning prefect, among them a fifteenth-century treasure: the Ile de la Cité's Nazareth Arch.

The Hôtel le Peletier de Saint-Fargeau features reconstituted period decors that illustrate a multiplicity of styles: ceilings and tapestries by Charles Le Brun; Louis XV and Louis XVI salons with pieces by Madame de Pompadour's furniture supplier Pierre Migeon, a grand, neoclassical military café, Marcel Proust's bedroom and no fewer than a dozen rooms dedicated to the French Revolution, each one lined with epoch-defining striped fabric. In addition, Marie-Antoinette's dressing table, medallions and fans are exhibited alongside etchings and paintings, as well as regal or revolutionary emblems and memorabilia, including the dauphin's dominoes and toy soldiers, a coffin-shaped ring containing some of his father's hair, the keys of the Bastille and some miniature guillotines.

Each historical era has its chroniclers and portraitists. The Musée Carnavalet's archives include precious documents. A painting by Hubert Robert depicts a scene at Paris's Saint-Lazarre prison that would have been familiar during the Revolution. Friends and relatives are shown handing food to its aristocratic occupants, who stretch over a stone balustrade to grab the offerings. The better-off brought extra supplies that were passed on to poorer prisoners who belonged to the impoverished nobility. Jean-Louis Prieur, like Jacques-Louis David, was one of the Revolution's most prolific artists, and produced distinctive wash drawings that depicted major events and highlighted various aspects of everyday life during the Terror. Prieur was to this period what the photographer Félix Nadar — otherwise known as the caricaturist Tournachon — would be to late nineteenth-century and early twentieth-century Paris: its eyes and memory.

Prieur's freehand sketches are as representative of the revolutionary era's turmoil as Nadar's photographic pantheon of celebrities is evocative of *belle époque* optimism. Also in the Musée Carnavalet collection is *La veuve Capet*, an exceptional draughtsman's portrait of Marie-Antoinette incarcerated in the Conciergerie. Equally eloquent is David's well-known pen-and-ink drawing of the condemned queen sitting in the cart that carried her to the scaffold, her hands tied behind her back, which belongs to the Louvre.

In contrast to these haunting images are French genre paintings, which enjoyed their heyday around the same time. While Jean-Baptiste-Siméon Chardin — a true Parisian, born in 1699 — concentrated on interiors that enhanced the daily existence of ordinary people, Antoine Watteau and Jean Honoré Fragonard were the uncontested masters of depicting an aristocratically bucolic way of life that provided a playful counterpoint to the Age of Enlightenment's philosophical divergences, which were destined eventually to trigger the Revolution. Sadly, Watteau — less frivolous than his subject matter implies — succumbed to consumption in his early thirties.

Soothed by the music of the court's official composer, Jean Baptiste Lully, the Sun King's retinue had no desire to face reality.

The eighteenth century also had Madame de Pompadour and her protégés: the architect Ange-Jacques Gabriel, the carpenter Jean-François Oeben, the sculptor Jean-Baptiste Pigalle, and a bevy of painters, including François Boucher, Latour, Jean-Marc Nattier and Carle Vanloo. Salons were held in sumptuous *hôtels particuliers*, where sharp-witted women entertained the leading lights of the Age of Enlightenment (Voltaire, Marivaux, Montesquieu, Jean-Jacques Rousseau), and in cafés, such as Le Procope, contributors to Denis Diderot's illustrated *Encyclopédie* met to discuss everything from science to art in a philosophical light. Here they often drank coffee or chocolate – exotic beverages that had become fashionable in the previous century, when Madame de Sévigné had commented on them in her letters after their properties had been tested at the Jardin des Plantes botanical garden, created under Louis XIII. The eighteenth century also had pamphleteers, caricaturists and free-thinking libertines enamoured of erotic literature.

Then, and in the seventeenth century, could the king and aristocrats at Versailles have heard the rumblings of discontent emanating from the city's mean streets? Soothed by the music of the court's official composer Jean Baptiste Lully, the Sun King's retinue had no desire to face reality, any more than did the next generation of courtiers, who listened to baroque masterpieces by François Couperin and Jean Philippe Rameau against a backdrop of pastoral genre scenes painted by Watteau, Fragonard or Boucher – the antithesis of the etchings of Jacques Callot, a seventeenth-century artist who focused on the plight of Parisian have-nots: beggars, crippled soldiers, itinerant actors and hospice patients.

Even before the French Revolution, there had been a tradition of urban protest in Paris that was part of a bigger picture: internecine conflict was latent there and in the country as a whole. The fourteenth century had seen *Jacqueries* (violent peasant revolts), and a bourgeois uprising led by the city's provost, Etienne Marcel. Time and again Paris has attempted to reinvent itself, refusing to take the fruit of its hard-fought past struggles for granted. If pollsters and spin doctors had existed, could they have warned the eighteenth century's Versailles-based monarchs, cut off from city life, that they were heading for tragedy – and would the monarchs have listened?

THE IMPERIAL DREAM

Now reappraisal was on the agenda and
Napoleon 1 was determined to turn the page,
envisioning his glorious contribution to as yet
unwritten chapters in the history of France.

Hot on the heels of a blood-spilling revolution that shook the foundations of medieval feudalism came an era during which the ambience of Paris changed radically. Spanning two empires and three republics, the nineteenth century was punctuated by popular uprisings and royalist comebacks; it was to witness extraordinary scientific advances that exerted a major influence on the arts.

At the outset of the First Republic, proclaimed in 1792, every institution of the *ancien régime* (old order) – ranging from the monarchy (associated with a spiral of financial ruin and absolutism that had started in the seventeenth century under Louis XIV) to apparently harmless words, such as 'monsieur' and 'madame', replaced by 'citoyen' and 'citoyenne' (citizen, male and female) – had been abolished. And a republican calendar that renamed each month of the year replaced the Christian one. For example, in 1804 Napoleon Bonaparte was crowned Emperor of France not in plain old December, but in far more poetic Frimaire (from *frimas* or 'frosty winter weather').

Now reappraisal was on the agenda and Napoleon I was determined to turn the page, envisioning his glorious contribution to as yet unwritten chapters in the history of France. But the road towards the institutionalization of revolutionary values, which the emperor saw happening at home as well as abroad in the territories he conquered, was to be a bumpy one. As certain observers analysing the causes of the 2005 *banlieue* riots in the outer suburbs of France's cities have suggested, then, as in present-day Paris, the population appeared to be 'more gifted for revolution than reform'.

When their new masters set out to redesign the capital and how it was run, its citizens took to the streets, suspecting them of replanning its boulevards and rationalizing its administrative structures in order to curb potential dissent. The elegant avenues, along which Parisian *flâneurs* (strollers) love to amble nowadays – pausing to sit in one of the city's characteristic pavement cafés and watch the world go by while they sip a cup of coffee or a cool draught beer –

The Republican Calendar

A relatively harmless by-product of the French Revolution was the republican calendar. Totally divested of religious references, it was adopted in 1793 and abolished by Napoleon in 1806 (although fleetingly reinstated by the Paris Commune of 1871). Curiously, it put the clock back, counting each year in Roman numerals from 22 September 1792, the first day of year one of the Republic.

Based on ten months of equal length (with three ten-day weeks, or 'decades', each straddled across two of the traditional Gregorian calendar's months), it featured a leap-year day every four years and ended with five additional solar days dubbed *sans culottides* – meaning 'the days of the *sans-culottes*' (days dedicated to the poorest and fiercest revolutionaries who wore full-length trousers or pants, as opposed to aristocratic knee-breeches).

As it happens, the calendar's 'politically correct' months were more 'poetically correct' than might be expected. *Germinal* (the title of Emile Zola's famous 1885 novel) is a nod to the 'sowing season' (March–April), while *Brumaire* evokes Napoleon-Bonaparte's 1799 coup d'état (the subject of Karl Marx's 1852 pamphlet entitled *The 18th Brumaire of Louis Napoleon*), which took place in 'misty' October–November. *Brumaire* being an allusion to *brume*, French for 'mist'.

ABOVE The Republican Calendar for 1793, with each day named after a seed, fruit, tool, animal, tree or flower.

were perceived as a threat. Why were these newfangled thoroughfares so wide? Was it to keep disorderly crowds under control in the event of an insurrection? The discrepancy between the means deployed to achieve this metamorphosis, with medieval buildings demolished and communities scattered, and the miserable, unimproved living conditions of the city's have-nots was too great. Bitter revolts ensued in the middle of the century. However, the good news in these ground-breaking times, which saw the emergence of heated political debates pursued in cafés and newspapers, was that at the end of the tunnel there was a glimmer of (electric) light.

Towards the turn of the nineteenth century, Paris enjoyed a period of intense creativity. Marked by Expositions Universelles (World Fairs) that announced industrial innovations, and boosted by the invention of electricity, the *belle époque* (beautiful era) heralded a series of – bloodless – artistic and technological revolutions, from the monumental metallic architecture of Gustave Eiffel's tower to Art Nouveau and Impressionism, documented by pioneering photographers. Electric lighting opened up a whole new world of after-dark activities: Paris by night was born.

Above all, this enthralling century, torn between the desire to innovate and the paradoxical need to redefine its own social conventions, is personified by one of history's most iconic figures. Napoleon Bonaparte has inspired more feature films and plays than any of his counterparts. His meteoric rise to power, his military conquests and his spectacular defeats are the stuff of Hollywood blockbusters. Beyond the obvious stereotype of the short politician driven by huge personal ambitions, this visionary

empire builder, who dreamt of converting Paris into a city as grandiose as ancient Rome – 'the most beautiful that ever existed, but also the most beautiful that could ever exist' – had star quality.

With his hand-in-waistcoat pose and bicorne hat, Napoleon I is remembered not only as a controversial and flamboyant leader brought to his knees by chimerical imperial campaigns, but, perhaps even more, as an astute administrator who made concrete contributions to the management of his country. He divided France into regions, called *départements*, and appointed prefects to administer them, a system that continues to this day, while the Napoleonic Code remains the basis of our legal system.

Naturally, it is impossible to portray nineteenth-century Paris without paying particular attention to Napoleon III's architect–prefect Baron Georges Haussmann, who gave the capital a totally new look, replacing its bucolic *faubourgs* (outskirts) with neo-classical tree-lined boulevards.

LEFT Paris seen from the Tour Montparnasse skyscraper, on a cloudy afternoon. The capital's modern constructions and Haussmannian buildings compete for attention with medieval monuments – such as the Church of Saint-Sulpice (bottom right).

The Dreyfus Affair

French society is highly codified, not least our educational system and its *grandes écoles* (élitist superschools). The Ecole Polytechnique relies on code numbers to identify its alumni, adding the letter X followed by the year of their graduation to their names. The roll-call of graduates of the Polytechnique ranges from prominent nineteenth-century figures, such as Fulgence Bienvenüe (X1870), the civil engineer who oversaw the construction of Paris's Métro, to the twentieth-century President, Valéry Giscard d'Estaing (X1944). A former student of the Polytechnique was temporarily discredited, after reaching the highest echelons: Captain Alfred Dreyfus (X1878), the army officer at the centre of the 'Dreyfus Affair'.

Dreyfus was accused of supplying military secrets to Germany in 1894, but the charges brought against him were inspired more by anti-Semitism than hard evidence. So apparent was the injustice of his trial and imprisonment that the novelist Emile Zola wrote an open letter to President Felix Faure entitled *J'Accuse*. Published on the front page of the daily newspaper *L'Aurore* in January 1898, it angrily exposed attempts to cover up official mistakes. When finally completely exonerated of the false accusations levelled against him, Dreyfus was reinstated to the military and awarded the Legion of Honour.

ABOVE Alfred Dreyfus (1859–1935), the Jewish military officer arrested for treason in 1894.

BELOW Emile Zola's open letter to the French president, published in *L'Aurore*, accusing the authorities of a cover-up.

The New Order

Napoleon I had a clear view of his personal destiny, seeing it as part of a bigger chronological picture. He believed that leaders were only as great as the monuments they left behind. The Arc de Triomphe, which dominates the Champs-Elysées like a Roman arch, was built at his instigation, as was the star-shaped place de l'Etoile (now place Charles de Gaulle), which was completed by Napoleon III.

In the middle of the place Vendôme, famed for its luxury jewellers clustered around the Ritz Hotel, stands a perfect example of the tokens of grandeur he envisaged: a lookalike of Trajan's Column in Rome, with Napoleon himself on top of it, posing as Julius Caesar. The column is decorated with scenes representing the high points of this self-styled icon's illustrious military career.

To display the spoils of his empire, most of which were returned to their original owners in 1815 after the Battle of Waterloo, Napoleon refurbished the Louvre and built its north wing. Once the residence of Francis I, an eminent patron of the great masters of the Italian Renaissance, whose collection included Leonardo da Vinci's *Mona Lisa*, the former palace had begun its career as the world's most famous museum in 1793, when the doors of its Grande Galerie were first opened to visitors.

Like the Bourbon kings before him, and not unlike some of today's media-conscious politicians, Napoleon I fostered the arts partly to cultivate his own image. The least that can be said was that he had a sense of *mise en scène* epitomized by his commissioning one of the Louvre's chief attractions: Jacques Louis David's monumental painting of his coronation, which was staged in the most sacred symbol of Paris: Notre-Dame Cathedral. I would normally walk straight past this type of official composition but, fortunately for us, David was by no means a fawning sycophant. I find it endearing that he decided to depict Napoleon crowning the Empress Joséphine instead of concentrating on the emperor's consecration.

Although he had been the Revolution's official artist–propagandist, designing the costumes and décor for Robespierre's Festival of the Supreme Being, David definitely had a mind of his own. A champion of neoclassicism, he managed to provide a fresh take on even the most unlikely subject matter. In 1793 he had risen to the challenge of illustrating the gruesome circumstances surrounding the assassination of Jean Paul Marat. Killed in his bathtub by Charlotte Corday, this protagonist of the Reign of Terror (see page 83) – an influential journalist who published radical editorials in *L'Ami du peuple* (The Friend of the People) – was accustomed to making notes while bathing to obtain relief from a skin disease. The result of David's forbidding assignment? A realistic if idealized depiction of political martyrdom as disturbing as any paparazzi reportage.

In E. H. Gombrich's *The Story of Art* (1950), a book on the reading list of art students all over the world, the author describes the revolutionaries of this epic epoch as 'Greeks and Romans reborn', observing that, 'These people felt that they were living in heroic times, and that the events of their own

years were just as worthy of the painter's attention as the episodes of Greek or Roman history.'

In 1802, in tune with this thinking, Napoleon instituted the Legion of Honour. Still top of the French honours list, this prestigious decoration, which can be awarded to any person regardless of social rank, became a model for other orders of merit. The legendary Corsican was himself an exemplar for recipients of this award – a brilliant, young general whose career had started with a scholarship to the Ecole Militaire, the military academy in Paris founded by Madame de Pompadour, and who had made the leap from first consul installed by *coup d'état* to emperor crowned after a landslide referendum in his favour.

Fascinated by hierarchy, and a firm believer in discipline and meritocracy, he instigated the notoriously competitive *lycée* (grammar-school) system, beginning with the Lycée Henri IV (known as HIV – H Four), whose twentieth-century alumni include the Front Populaire leader Léon Blum and the philosopher Jean-Paul Sartre. (The latter went on to attend the Lycée Louis-le-Grand [LLG, named after Louis XIV] and the Ecole Normale Supérieure on the rue d'Ulm – a hat trick in terms of academic achievement.)

ABOVE Place Charles de Gaulle, at dusk. No fewer than twelve avenues radiate from this star-shaped intersection, formerly known as the place de l'Etoile, with the Arc de Triomphe at its centre.

The magnificent Arc de Triomphe and the star-shaped Place de l'Etoile were built at the instigation of Napoleon 1, who believed that leaders were only as great as the monuments they left behind.

Situated in the heart of the Latin Quarter, Paris's historical student district since Robert de Sorbon founded the Sorbonne in 1257, HIV and LLG are top *lycées*. Perched on the Montagne Sainte-Geneviève, a slope dominated by the Panthéon – the temple-like mausoleum that is the final resting place of such great Frenchmen as Voltaire and André Malraux, and for the moment just one woman (Marie Curie) – these rigorously selective state schools are regarded as pinnacles of scholastic excellence. They are part of a network of educational establishments that prepare successive generations of hand-picked whizz-kids for the *grandes écoles*, crème de la crème superschools that continue to feed France's public and private sectors with future decision-makers, and that have produced countless numbers of eminent politicians, diplomats and authors, often laureates of the Prix de l'Académie Goncourt. The jury for this leading literary prize, created at the turn of the century and yet another bastion of Parisian cultural life, deliberates *chez* Drouant. Originally one of the capital's first bar-tabacs, opened in 1880 by Charles Drouant, a native of Alsace, this old-established restaurant was the favourite haunt of artists such as Auguste Renoir, Camille Pissarro and Auguste Rodin.

France's flagship *grande école*, the Polytechnique, was originally a military academy. On Bastille Day (14 July) and other special occasions cadets are seen on television parading along the Champs-Elysées in the school's *grand uniforme* (nicknamed '*grand u*'). This has a strikingly elegant Napoleonic look: dark trousers or skirt with a red stripe, brass buttons, bicorne hat and sword. Established during the French Revolution, and originally called the Ecole Centrale des Travaux Publics (Central School of Public Works), it was renamed the Ecole Polytechnique before Napoleon moved it to Montagne Sainte-Geneviève in 1804. No longer a military school, in spite of the uniform, it is a state-subsidized civilian institution, run under the auspices of the Ministry of Defence. In 1976 its campus was transferred to Palaiseau, approximately 24 kilometres (15 miles) from Paris.

Sadly, Napoleon I's role in the history of France was not emulated by his son, the child of his marriage to the Austrian archduchess Marie-Louise (he divorced Joséphine because she failed to give him an heir). Napoleon II, nicknamed 'L'Aiglon' (the Eaglet), was France's emperor for just a few days, even though his father abdicated twice in his favour – following defeat at Leipzig in 1813 (after which he was exiled to the island of Elba before staging his celebrated Hundred Days comeback) and Waterloo in 1815. In the second instance Parisian parliamentarians recognized the 'infant emperor' as Bonaparte's successor, but their decision was reversed when the allies (Austria, Prussia and Russia) entered the capital.

In a curious twist of fate, neither father nor son enjoyed a happy ending. The emperor apparent was relegated to splendid isolation in his mother's native country, where he was known as Franz, Duke of Reichstadt, until his death from tuberculosis at the age of twenty-one.

For Napoleon himself, who had marched past the Palais Royal as a penniless cadet, counting on a brilliant military career peppered with feats of arms to propel him towards grander designs, having to surrender Paris after his defeat at Leipzig was most certainly the ultimate outrage. On 31 March 1814 Charles Talleyrand, the cleric and statesman who led the opposition to him, had handed the keys of the capital to Tsar Alexander I, obliging the emperor to abdicate unconditionally.

The allied armies re-entered the city in 1815, after Napoleon's last stand at Waterloo. In what the population of Paris must have experienced as a mockery of Napoleonic order, the dreaded Cossacks were to be seen bivouacking on the Champs-Elysées and drying their shirts and trousers on the railings of the Tuileries Palace. Be that as it may, there was a positive consequence to the Russian occupation. As *les Russes* rushed from one tavern to the next demanding to be fed instantly, *'Bistro! Bistro!'* ('Quickly! Quickly!'), they were unwittingly naming a type of restaurant that is for ever linked with the Parisian way of life.

Napoleon's imposing red-quartzite tomb, under the dome of Les Invalides, seems almost smug, like a posthumous snub to the exiled emperor's detractors, and is a testimonial to the survival of the new order he endeavoured to implement on all fronts. Many of

OPPOSITE *La Barrière de Clichy, Défense de Paris* (The Gate at Clichy during the Defence of Paris), *30 March 1814* (1820) by Emile Jean Horace Vernet.

France's renowned war heroes are also buried in the monument, along with Rouget de l'Isle, the writer and composer of the Marseillaise, the country's stridently revolutionary national anthem. The music was later rearranged by Hector Berlioz.

Opposing Reactions

What an eventful century – not so much in perpetual motion, as in a state of constant instability. Echoing Sir Isaac Newton's theory that every action produces an equal but opposite reaction, the implementation of republicanism was stalled by intermittent attempts to restore the monarchy, which sparked popular unrest. In sharp contrast to Napoleon's reorganizing of every-

thing from the nation's legal and educational systems to its finances – he commissioned the architect Alexandre Théodore Brongniart to build the Palais de la Bourse (stock exchange) – France became increasingly volatile after the emperor's downfall. From one change of government to the next, Paris was the scene of ruthlessly repressed uprisings that left deep scars.

Louis XVIII, the younger brother of Louis XVI, had acceded to the French throne in 1814. He established a constitutional monarchy and, after a brief interruption when Napoleon returned from Elba, ruled until 1824. In 1830 the ultra-royalist regime of the Restoration's second king, Louis's brother Charles X, was cut short by the Trois Glorieuses (July

Revolution), which takes its French name from the three glorious days of 27, 28 and 29 July that led to the more bourgeois than regal 'July monarchy' of Louis-Philippe.

The reign of this irreverently caricatured 'citizen–king' came to an end in the spring of 1848, when a wave of revolutionary idealism swept across Europe in the midst of a severe economic crisis. Prior to his abdication, riots had broken out in the capital and had been brutally quashed, causing further discontent. Triggered in February, France's two-part Revolution led to the proclamation of a Second Republic, remembered for establishing universal suffrage for men, and for securing the abolition of slavery. Within months of these decrees, more barricades were erected. Sadly, the outcome of part two of Paris's participation in what

became known as the 'spring of nations' or 'people's spring' dashed the hopes of advocates of a republican government with social priorities. The June Days Uprising finished in tragedy, with 50,000 insurgents under siege in the *faubourgs* (inner suburbs). Hearing of the troops' actions against the city's mainly under-nourished and unemployed population, the novelist George Sand declared she was 'ashamed to be French' and no longer believed in a republic that 'begins by killing its proletarians'.

Next in the nineteenth-century timeline comes a political milestone that prompted Victor Hugo, the politically committed Romantic writer par excellence, to go into exile: President Louis-Napoleon Bonaparte's political takeover. Adieu Second Republic, enter the Second Empire, ruled by Napoleon III. On 2 December 1851 the forty-seventh anniversary of the coronation of his uncle Napoleon I, the freshly constituted republic's democratically elected leader mounted what has since been termed a 'self-coup' and overthrew his own government. Then, exactly a year after he'd stormed the National Assembly, he appointed himself emperor.

On each occasion he held a referendum, designed to validate his actions, and both of these plebiscites were crowned with landslide victories. Within months of his coup, Napoleon's nephew polled the French people. Did they want to be governed by him? Were they willing to empower him to establish a constitution? 'Yes,' replied the vast majority of Frenchmen. So be it. In January 1852, following in the footsteps of his relative Napoleon the Great, Louis-Napoleon moved

into the Tuileries Palace, set on creating a hereditary imperial state. By November this dream had become a reality – an even greater number of voters had given his accession to imperial status the people's seal of approval.

Nevertheless, in December 1851 the rue Beaubourg had been the scene of violent repression when opponents to the coup, who had mounted barricades in the area, were the target of summary executions. This is the same street – formerly the rue Transnonain – that, nearly twenty years earlier, in April 1834, had been the site of a massacre recorded in a drawing by Honoré Daumier. Soldiers who had heard gunfire in

ABOVE LEFT *Rue Transnonain, 15 April 1834.* In this drawing, disseminated as a lithograph shortly after the event, the caricaturist Honoré Daumier expressed his indignation at civilian killings perpetrated on the rue Transnonain (now the rue Beaubourg). **ABOVE RIGHT** *Agonie de la Commune, derniers combats dans le Cimetière du Père-Lachaise* (Agony of the Commune, last

fights in the Cemetery of Père-Lachaise), an engraving by L. J. A. Daudenarde from *Le Monde illustré*, 27 May 1871. In a tragic episode that marked the end of the Paris Commune of 1871, the last of the insurrectional government's staunchest supporters (known as the Communards) were lined up and shot at the Père-Lachaise cemetery, before being buried on the spot.

the dark entered a building (number 12) and opened fire on its inhabitants, killing entire families. Fortunately, few visitors to the Pompidou Centre (at number 19) are aware of this bygone carnage.

Two decades after the coup, at the time of France's defeat in the Franco-Prussian War, the bourgeois aspirations and colonialist objectives championed by Napoleon III's empire were largely disavowed. In 1871, once again in springtime, an urban uprising resulted in the creation of the Paris Commune. The name was not new as it had been applied to the revolutionary government that was in power until 1795, but no matter – this is the Paris Commune everyone remembers. Strictly speaking, it was nothing more than a local authority that officiated for two or three months. In the aftermath of the siege preceding their city's capitulation, and angered by the ensuing token 'ceremonial' Prussian occupation, starving Parisians protested, requesting a '*république démocratique et sociale*' (democratic socialist republic) in keeping with revolutionary principles. They wanted Paris to be self-governing, like its regional counterparts.

Proclaimed on 28 March 1871, the Commune temporarily brought back the revolutionary calendar and substituted the red flag for the less radical red, white and blue *tricolore*. Crushed by Louis-Philippe's former prime minister Adolphe Thiers, it was the catalyst in a poignant political episode that left a crucial imprint on Paris. Tens of thousands of its advocates were shot on sight, imprisoned, or faced with deportation. Curiously, a doyen of the movement, Louis Auguste Blanqui – after whom a boulevard in the 13th arrondissement is named – was elected president of the Commune in his absence. Thanks to being under arrest throughout the whole proceedings, he was out of harm's way.

Feminists came to the fore, consolidating the efforts of their 1789 sisters. An anarchist and proud of it, Louise Michel (also known as the 'red virgin of Montmartre') was seen as a living emblem of revolutionary liberty and embodies the spirit of Eugène Delacroix's landmark painting *La Liberté guidant le peuple* (Liberty Leading the People). Although deported to New Caledonia in the South Pacific, she eventually returned to Paris when an amnesty was granted to the Communards. An ambulance-woman who had elected to join the National Guard, the Pasionaria of the emerging French workers' movement continued to inspire popular sympathy long after her death in 1905. In the build-up to the First World War demonstrators gathered around her tomb, expressing their respect for this ardent supporter of the Paris Commune.

The ferocity of the Commune's outcome is nowhere more vivid than at the Père-Lachaise cemetery, in front of the Mur des Fédérés (Wall of Federationists), against which the last remaining Communards, 147 in all, were lined up and shot, then interred on the spot in a common grave. The anniversary of this tragic episode, which marked the conclusion of the uprising, continues to be commemorated each year on 28 May. Sympathizers deposit wreaths, while others visitors – there purely by chance, to commune with Edith Piaf or Jim Morrison – gaze incredulously at the bullet holes in the wall.

In 1873, as France embarked on a Third Republic with a soldier-president, Patrice de Macmahon, Duke of Magenta – no friend of republicanism – at its head, the spectre of military repression hovered over the streets of Paris.

In the light of the Commune and the 1830 and 1848 springtime insurrections, the phrase 'Paris in the spring' takes on a significance different from the one sung about in popular song. In fact, 1 May is International Workers' Day and has a special dimension in our capital. On this public holiday, which – mysteriously – tends to be blessed with sunny weather, street vendors set up stalls on the boulevards to sell

OPPOSITE Traditionally, Bastille Day demonstrators march from the Colonne de Juillet at the centre of the place de la Bastille, to this monument on the place de la République. Unveiled on 14 July 1880, it's a tribute to the republican ideals, and the bronze lion at its base stands for universal suffrage.

sprigs of lily of the valley, said to bring good luck. Meanwhile, politicians join the ranks of banner-holding workers and union leaders to take part in generally good-humoured May Day demonstrations. As they march past the place de la République's 45-metre (150-foot) column commemorating the 1830 and 1848 revolts, some people will think of Louise Michel (or even one of France's chart-topping bands, Louise Attaque, which is named after her), others of the riots of May 1968.

In the not-so-distant past, the spring of 2006, when students obtained the withdrawal of the law that gave employers the right to dismiss young workers without justification during the first two years of a job contract, television viewers saw Julie Coudry, president of France's Confédération Etudiante (Student Confederation), sporting a *gavroche* cap (a reminder of the urchin in Victor Hugo's *Les Misérables*). Perhaps spring in Paris has a special ingredient that predestines the city to bring out the romantic hero in all of us – the idealist who wants to make a difference.

Monumental Makeover

Throughout the stirring events of the second part of the century, the Industrial Revolution gained momentum. Like the steam engine in Claude Monet's world-famous painting of Saint-Lazare in the Musée d'Orsay – itself originally a mainline station, inaugurated during the Exposition Universelle of 1900 – Haussmannian Paris was all set to forge ahead, envisaging modernism as a vector of prosperity. In spite of the ongoing push and pull between the population's

desperate bids to secure social and economic reforms, and the recurrent military repression exerted by the period's different regimes, the nineteenth century would end *en beauté* (in beauty) – in a flourish of *belle époque* innovation. The hard-earned effervescence of the 'beautiful era' was recorded on camera, thanks to the advent of photography and moving pictures. At the dawn of the automotive age (Peugeot devised its first automobile – a three-wheeled, steam-powered vehicle pioneered in collaboration with Léon Serpollet – in the late 1880s) early film-makers would document the bustling atmosphere of a *fin de siècle* capital proudly showcasing its technological advances.

Much like any household – at once exhilarated and disconcerted by a move or change of decor – Paris suffered a culture shock when Napoleon III's town-planning prefect, Georges Eugène Haussmann undertook his *grands travaux* (great works). More than a decade before the invention of the pneumatic drill, his architects and engineers picked up where Napoleon I had left off. Bonaparte had put the rue de Rivoli in front of the Tuileries Palace. Now the Second Empire would create gigantic axes, piercing the city from east to west and north to south. For a little over ten years, its rat-infested and barricade-friendly alleyways were a complete shambles. Baron Haussmann was convinced that the sole solution to the old city's woes was a blank-canvas approach that would give its citizens a fresh start, so he went for a total look, demolishing edifices that were vital to the social fabric of the community.

In the name of renovation he did not hesitate to

ABOVE This huge clock reminds visitors to the Musée d'Orsay of its origins as a railway station. Prior to its most recent metamorphosis as a museum highlighting nineteenth-century art, the building served several purposes and inspired film-makers, including Orson Welles, who used it for his adaptation of Kafka's *The Trial* (1963).

formerly a railway station, the Musée d'Orsay, inaugurated on 14 July 1900, is a shining example of the monumental metallic architecture in vogue in Paris at the turn of the nineteenth century.

revamp the Ile de la Cité, going so far as to tear down fortifications constructed in the Middle Ages. Neither churches nor theatres were spared. The boulevard du Temple, near the place de la République, was a kind of disparate theatreland filled with multifarious establishments that presented all kinds of acts, from melodramatic tragedies to mime, juggling and comedy. It was jokingly labelled the 'boulevard du Crime', not because there were more gangs of what newspapers would soon call 'Apaches' (young hooligans) there than anywhere else, but because many of the productions staged in its vicinity were macabre whodunnits involving plots with multiple stabbings and killings. Sweeping this folklore aside, Haussmann's all-embracing plan shifted the focus elsewhere, and he commissioned Gabriel Davioud, the architect responsible for his boulevard's distinctive fittings (lampposts, kiosks and fountains), to erect two symmetrical theatres on the place du Châtelet.

RIGHT Situated in the Observatory garden, within steps of Saint-Sulpice church, the Fontaine des quatres mondes (Fountain of the Four Worlds) was built in 1746 to provide water for the area's wealthy residents.

around the personality of Sarah Bernhardt including the title role in *Fedora*, the light comedy that gave its name to a style of hat later favoured by Greta Garbo.

On Paris's tree-lined *grands boulevards*, such as boulevard des Italiens and boulevard des Capucines, theatres and opera houses popped up offering a fresh palette of light-hearted entertainment, from comedy to operettas. So-called *théâtre de boulevard* comedies became permanent fixtures in Parisian life. The ancestors of the television sitcoms that rely heavily on canned laughter, these unsophisticated but thoroughly codified pastiches of bourgeois existence have remained popular. Audiences love them because they know exactly what to expect. Top of the bill among the stereotypes that keep coming back in these well-oiled farces is the lord of the manor who cheats on his snooty wife with the maid and gets caught with his pants down, best exemplified in Georges Feydeau's first triumph, *Monsieur Chasse*.

Perhaps the only pre-Haussmannian playhouse in the area to have escaped this monumental makeover, the TLP (Théatre Libertaire de Paris, also known as Théatre Déjazet) possesses a unique decor that features walls painted with caricatures in the style of Honoré Daumier. Initially an eighteenth-century tennis court, it was transformed first into a bathhouse, then into a ballroom, before becoming a fully fledged theatre in 1842. Its founder, Virginie Déjazet, was a popular actress who excelled in 'courtier' and 'valet' parts that required breeches, which came to be known as *Déjazets*. She contributed to the success of the dramatist Victorien Sardou, introducing him to her theatre-world connections early in his career. Sardou specialized in a nineteenth-century genre that critics came to define as the solid, well-made play. In this spirit he came up with a number of characters built

ABOVE LEFT Sarah Bernhardt (1844–1923), the greatest *tragédienne* of her day, relaxing in her salon. Born in Paris, she found fame on the stages of Europe in the 1870s, and was soon in demand in the United States. The celebrated Art Nouveau artist, Alphons Mucha, designed several posters representing her.

OPPOSITE The ornate grand staircases of Paris's Palais Garnier opera house converge, continuing to impress modern-day visitors with their Napoleonic sense of splendour.

ABOVE The Art Deco cupola of Printemps department store was recently renovated, to the delight of shoppers lunching at its chic rooftop restaurant. The sphere in the centre is a globe-shaped film screen.

After laughing their heads off for a couple of hours, nineteenth-century theatre-goers were in the mood for food. Hence the profusion of cafés and restaurants that sprang up in and around these new-style play-houses. The district surrounding Paris's flourishing Palais Brongniart *bourse* (stock exchange) became equally *à la mode*. On the corner of the rue de la Bourse and rue Vivienne, right next to the Agence France-Presse news agency, the Vaudeville brasserie is as bub-bly as ever. In another life it was the bar of the theatre where in 1852 the younger Alexandre Dumas staged an adaptation of his novel *La Dame aux camélias* (The Lady of the Camellias). (The play is known as *Camille* in English.) Alas, the theatre was demolished at the turn of the century to make way for the rue du Quatre-Septembre, but the Vaudeville remains one of the only Parisian brasseries to have authentic 1930s Art Deco furnishings by the Solvet brothers; the other two are La Closerie des Lilas and La Coupole. Close your eyes when a luncheon service is in full swing in this lively establishment, where spruce business executives and frivolous fashionistas mingle, and you can easily pic-ture two-timing *demi-mondaines* (kept women) of the *belle époque*, camped by 'boulevard' playwrights, alight-ing from their carriages and throwing themselves into the arms of their paramours, chuckling coquettishly as they think up excuses for their tardiness.

On the subject of horse-drawn vehicles, I'm told the reason why French actors say, *'Merde!'* ('Shit!') to each other — corresponding to the English 'Break a leg!' — before they go on stage is that if a show was well received, carriages and hansom cabs would line up in

front of the theatre in large numbers. The more spectators who turned up, the greater the quantity of manure deposited at the entrance.

Charles Garnier's Palais Garnier, commissioned by Napoleon III, is paramount among the architectural delights of the Second Empire that invariably, as if by magic, impress their Napoleonic magnetism on visitors to modern-day Paris. It was the city's one and only opera house until François Mitterrand, France's first socialist president after the Second World War, called upon Carlos Ott, a Montevideo-born architect established in Canada, to provide the 9th arrondissement's baroque masterpiece with a Bastille-based alter ego – a virtual extension on the other side of town.

Although the Palais Garnier's initial foundation stone was laid in 1861, the opera house was not officially inaugurated until 15 January 1875. Numerous practical problems arose because of the marshy nature of the soil under the 12,000 square-metre (130,000 square-foot) site, and these, combined with a succession of historical upheavals – the Franco-Prussian War, the Paris Commune and, of course, the fall of the empire in 1870 – put the brakes on this ambitious project, set in motion by the century's second emperor.

Parisians who skirt the building on foot or by car after a shopping spree in boulevard Haussmann's Printemps and Galeries Lafayette department stores – also part of the capital's grand transformation – are at times awe-struck by its aura, as if they had never seen it before. Andrew Lloyd Webber's 1986 musical *The Phantom of the Opera* took its cue from Gaston Leroux's novel, which was serialized in *Le Gaulois* from September 1909 to January 1910. On my backstage visit to the Palais Garnier, I was told there really is a house ghost. Legend has it that the opera house got off to a bad start when a chandelier fell on a woman in the

ABOVE The Galeries Lafayette. The glass cupolas of Paris's first *grands magasins* (department stores) are supposed to have been conceived so that the goods on sale would be showered with light, rendering them irresistible to potential customers.

audience. To this day, the seat she was sitting in is always left empty.

Behind the scenes, this richly adorned edifice is akin to a real-life film set, with its costume racks bursting with period attire and rehearsal rooms hidden behind thick doors. Visiting the tank in the basement, adjacent to the building's old stables, is a spooky experience, even in the company of the technicians who work there every day. It's hard to think of it simply as a piece of plumbing that was installed as a safety measure by engineers keen to get started on the foundations; after eight months of uninterrupted pumping they had been unable to stop a constant flow of water from seeping out of the ground. What if the tank was indeed a murky lake, the phantom's lair?

As if the underground tank weren't enough to get the imagination going, the Palais Garnier is 'haunted' by rats. To be precise, by *petits rats* (little rats), the name given to the tutu-clad 'little mice' who learnt to dance *en pointe* at the Paris Opera Ballet School before they entered the corps de ballet. They are no longer trained in this ornate marble monument, where the plush velvet seating, gold-leaf trimmings, stately statuary and lofty columns must have been intimidating for beginners entering the holy of holies in the footsteps of their idols. In the late 1980s their school was transferred to modern premises on the southern outskirts of Paris. Even so, they perform in the opera house at different stages of their careers, and all of them continue to entertain the same dream: some day something fabulous, something they've always been waiting for, will happen under Garnier's pastel-hued

dome, painted by Marc Chagall in 1964. Some day they will be named *danseuse étoile* (a star dancer). This glowing vision is the reward for relentless daily exertion, as depicted by the Impressionist Edgar Degas, who was fascinated by the harsh reality underlying the pretty spectacle of dance.

The Palais Garnier is by no means the only example of Napoleon III's vision for Paris. A fervent Anglophile, he had been charmed by the rosy cheeks of children he'd seen at play on one of his trips to London. The emperor attributed their healthy complexions to the profusion of parks he'd encountered in the British capital. Anxious that Parisian infants should benefit from fresh air in the same way, he instructed Baron Haussmann to conceive similar leafy open spaces, designed to be the lungs of Paris. These included the Bois de Boulogne to the south of the city,

OPPOSITE *La classe de Danse* (1873–6), a dancing class study by Edgar Degas.

and the Bois de Vincennes on its southwestern borders. The largest of the leafy havens in central Paris is the Parc des Buttes-Chaumont, just to the west of Montmartre. Once the site of gallows and a rubbish tip, it had a grim reputation before it was converted into a whimsical pleasure garden, complete with picturesque bridges and winding paths, a lake and a waterfall, and a grotto with faux stalactites – ready for the Exposition Universelle of 1867. To this day, actors and singers keen to keep their voices in mint condition frequently choose to live in the Buttes area because of its high altitude and cleaner air.

To improve hygiene in the city, Napoleon III initiated a vast network of sewers, aqueducts and waterways that included the Canal de l'Ourcq. In addition, gas was installed in the spick-and-span freestone apartment buildings that lined well-lit boulevards, some of which were as much as 30 metres (100 feet) wide. These drastic changes were viewed with a degree of scepticism by circumspect city-dwellers accustomed to strolling from one part of town to another, accepting an entente cordiale between distinct architectural messages: from the Renaissance refinement of Pierre Lescot's Fontaine des Innocents, sculpted by Jean Goujon and Augustin Pajou (now near Les Halles Métro station) to the peerless, seventeenth-century elegance of François Mansart's place Vendôme. They had witnessed the construction of the fortifications raised to stave off the threat of invasion during Napoleon Bonaparte's ailing campaigns, and had been surprised by the breadth of the boulevard that Baron Haussmann's predecessor, Prefect Rambuteau, had

hollowed out, hacking his way through the city centre with a view to facilitating the circulation of the population and promoting commercial exchanges. But this thoroughfare – now the rue Rambuteau – was only half as wide as Haussmann's major axes. In the same way that Parisians chatting in bistros tend to come up with worrying political scenarios after a few glasses of wine, a conspiracy theory gained ground slowly but surely in nineteenth-century café society. Supposing there was an ulterior motive behind the administration's desire to clean up the capital's derelict quarters?

Considering the magnitude of the urban alterations the Second Empire was imposing on the city, financing them with heavy expenditure and resorting to massive expulsions, Haussmann had been relatively popular. But the tide unexpectedly turned against him, and in a matter of days he became an outcast. A pamphlet by Jules Ferry, an up-and-coming reporter who would go down in history as a figurehead of republicanism, and who would later mastermind France's free, state-run educational system – lampooned him as a self-righteous upstart guilty of underhanded embezzlement. Even though it seems that Ferry's allegations were unfounded, his article could hardly pass unnoticed given its title: *Les Contes fantastiques de Haussmann* (Fantastic Tales of Haussmann). A witty allusion to the opera *The Tales of Hoffmann*, it was bound to attract attention at a time when phantasmagorical short stories by the likes of Guy de Maupassant were enjoying tremendous success. To add insult to injury, *contes* is a homonym, meaning both 'tales' and 'accounts'.

Heavy Metal

Paris's 'Stone Age', spearheaded by Napoleon III and Haussmann, would rapidly be supplanted by a futuristic 'Iron Age' whose architects were Gustave Eiffel and Victor-Louis Baltard. Less well known than Eiffel, Baltard dedicated two decades of his life (from 1852 to 1872) to *le ventre de Paris* (belly of Paris), a site that, like Covent Garden in London, existed to keep the city fed for more than a century. Both Parisians and tourists loved to visit this wholesale food market, called les Halles, in the wee hours of the morning, ending their expedition with a bowl of steaming onion soup. Sadly, most of its buildings were razed to the ground in the 1970s, but its pavilions were dismantled and rebuilt in Nogent-sur-Marne as the present Pavillon Baltard.

All young architects have a secret ambition to create a signature construction that makes them a big name in their lifetime and for generations to come. Having created the Eiffel Tower for the Exposition Universelle of 1889, as well as the inner metallic structure of the Statue of Liberty, Gustave Eiffel accomplished this dream on two occasions – and what is even more astonishing is that each of these

TOP RIGHT Built for the Exposition Universelle of 1889, the Eiffel Tower, which was originally highly controversial, has since become an international symbol of Paris.

CENTRE RIGHT The interior of the art-exhibition building constructed for the Exposition Universelle of 1889: sculptures on the ground floor, paintings on the balcony.

BOTTOM RIGHT Gustave Eiffel (1832–1933).

monuments has become a world-renowned symbol of the dreams represented by the city it was built for.

Iron really was the wonder material of the age, and it allowed architects to design buildings that were truly innovative. The 1900 Exposition Universelle spurred Paris's administrators to boost the capital's image by constructing glass and cast-iron exhibition halls that would be showcases for the technological advances that lay ahead. The Grand Palais and Petit Palais are fine examples. Art Nouveau in style, though classical in spirit, these 'instant monuments' – built at the same time as the Pont Alexandre III that faces them – have stood the test of time, although they were only recently reopened after extensive renovation. It was the second time the Grand Palais, inspired by London's Crystal Palace, had been repaired – the first was after it had been damaged during the Second World War. At the instigation of André Malraux, Charles de Gaulle's minister of culture, its northern wing initially housed the Galeries nationales du Grand Palais (a national gallery for temporary exhibitions). Over the years, its extensive hanging spaces have played host to numerous art exhibitions – a tradition reinstated for its September 2005 reopening, which coincided with the FIAC (Foire internationale de l'art contemporain) contemporary-art fair.

ABOVE LEFT The Pont Alexandre III and the glass-domed Grand Palais, which was inspired by London's Crystal Palace, both now splendidly restored. **ABOVE RIGHT** The Pont Alexandre III is one of Paris's most handsome bridges. Looking in the opposite direction, towards the Left Bank, visitors to the Grand Palais can catch a glimpse of Les Invalides military memorial and museum.

The 1900 Exposition Universelle also showcased the work of a virtuoso in the use of wrought iron: Hector Guimard, the Art Nouveau architect whose Métro station entrances have been an instantly recognizable feature of everyday life in the capital since Paris launched its underground transport system for the exhibition. Among the best examples of these are the glass-roofed entries at the Porte Dauphine and Abbesses stations. The subway exit leading to the Palais Garnier, however, isn't one of his. Fearing that a Guimard design would compete with the architecture of the opera house, town planners preferred to erect a stone stairway on this site.

An entrepreneurial concept that emerged around the turn of the nineteenth century was the idea of *grands magasins* (department stores). These shopping paradises, made of glass and cast iron, had a lot in common architecturally with the Grand Palais and Petit Palais, but the comparison stops there. They were emblematic of a brand-new development, namely, consumer culture. Emile Zola used the world's first one, the Bon Marché (built by Louis Charles Boileau in 1869, with the help of Gustave Eiffel), as a source of inspiration for his 1883 novel *Au Bonheur des Dames* (The Ladies' Delight). In this cautionary tale he examines the human and economic repercussions of such stores, relating the tragic destiny of a shopkeeper who faced unfair competition from a *grand magasin*.

A surviving example from the early days of department stores is Galeries Lafayette on boulevard Haussmann. Opened in 1908, it boasts a metallic roof that features a stained-glass cupola adorned with delightful floral motifs. This was allegedly conceived not merely for decorative purposes, but also so that the goods on sale would be showered with golden light, rendering them irresistible to potential customers.

Shopping became a fashionable activity, so much so that nineteenth-century store owners went to considerable lengths to attract a faithful clientele. Covered arcades suddenly appeared all over the city, the idea being that shoppers could pop into one store after another, regardless of the weather. Among the most intriguing is the chic, glass-roofed Galerie Vivienne (6 rue Vivienne). By way of comparison,

OPPOSITE AND ABOVE

A virtuoso in the use of wrought iron, the Art Nouveau architect Hector Guimard (1867–1942) left his mark on the capital with his distinctive Métro-station entrances.

Galerie Verot Dodat in the 1st arrondissement is worth a visit. In its early years it was always crowded because it was right next to the *terminus des diligences* (stage-coach depot).

Entering the Galerie Vivienne through one of its three entrances (at number 13 rue Vivienne), you'll find the staircase that leads to the home (unchanged since 1840) of François Vidocq, an ex-convict who became a bona-fide police chief at the head of a special brigade composed of ex-offenders. A friend and protector to many, Vidocq was apparently the inspiration for two characters in Victor Hugo's *Les Misérables*. According to Honoré de Balzac, he was a 'a great saver of souls'.

On a lighter note, you could finish your outing with a visit to the Théâtre des Bouffes Parisiens (Parisian Comic Opera Theatre), which is near Galerie Vivienne. Situated in passage Choiseul since 1826, this is where Jacques Offenbach's comic works were staged, and it remains home to them and many others in a similar vein.

LEFT (TOP AND BELOW)
Views of the Galerie Vivienne.
This typical nineteenth-century
Parisian *passage* (covered
shopping arcade) has mosaic
floors, palm trees, sculptures
and elegant shop fronts lining
skylit walkways that radiate from
a central atrium.

Café Society

With its beer and champagne bottles in the background, Edouard Manet's last major work – picturing a radiant barmaid serving clients at the Folies Bergère music hall – looks incredibly modern for a painting completed in 1882. Second Empire affluence had been good for business, even in Montmartre's red-light district, where the post-Impressionist painter Henri de Toulouse-Lautrec took lodgings in the late 1880s. Here he portrayed the district's working population in the raw, but without an ounce of contempt. Dancers, prostitutes, kept women enjoying a night out … each had their code and body language. In the crushed-velvet alcoves of its *lupanars* (a quaint literary term for lewd locales like these) a young lady removing her gloves was actually signalling her willingness to enter into a more intimate rapport with the dandy at her side. At the turn of the century, cafés and restaurants became hubs of city life, where male and female, money and politics all rubbed shoulders. Here top-hatted gentlemen, giving every appearance of simply having a good time, struck deals late into the night.

The ancestors of the terrace cafés that blossomed on Haussmann's boulevards amid the euphoria of the *belle époque* were the Age of Enlightenment coffee houses established in the build-up to the French Revolution. The very first of these eighteenth-century eating houses – Le Procope, just off the place de l'Odéon and still going strong – was soon followed by the Café de la Régence within the Palais Royal. Le Grand Véfour is another early restaurant that continues to attract an A-list clientele, and its *livre d'or* (visitors'

book) reads like a historical *Who's Who*. From Napoleon and Joséphine to the novelist Colette, who lived next door and dropped in as a neighbour, and from Jean-Paul Sartre to Juliette Greco, its dazzling period dining-rooms have seen political intrigues and celebrity romances for over 200 years. As the café has three Michelin stars, all this activity is accompanied by delicious food and rare vintages.

In the nineteenth century Paris was viewed as the hedonistic capital of the world. There were an estimated 30,000 sex workers in the city, and an amazing number of words were used to denote their status. For example, *camélia*, the name of a refined flower, was applied to 'tarts with a heart', as in the Alexandre Dumas novel *La Dame aux camélias* (The Lady of the Camellias), which was based on the real-life story of a certain Marie Duplessis. Such upmarket muses seduced their way to fame, fortune and power, and one of them – La Belle Otero – even had a salon at Lapérouse restaurant named after her.

A culinary sanctuary founded in 1766 at 51 quai des Grands-Augustins on the Left Bank, Lapérouse overlooks the Pont Neuf – famously misnamed as it's the oldest of our bridges – and was the first gourmet kitchen to receive a Michelin award, back in 1909. But there was more to this place than its delicious menu. Men of means could rendezvous here with their lady friends in the upstairs rooms, known as boudoir-lounges. The doors could be locked on the inside to prevent over-attentive waiters disturbing customers during their between-course encounters, and scratches on the mirrors were apparently made by courtesans

checking the quality of the diamonds offered to them by their wealthy companions. It's even rumoured that a tunnel links the establishment to the Senate, further along the Left Bank.

In an altogether different style, at Maxim's on the rue Royale, a special treat awaits fans of *belle époque* furniture and objets d'art: Pierre Cardin's *Collection 1900* is presented in a 'courtesan's apartment' filled with decorative *bibelots* (trinkets) by Daum and Emile Gallé. Style-setting restaurants like this temple of contemporary glamour became a highlight of Parisian life (toasted in Jacques Offenbach's 1866 operetta *La Vie Parisienne*). Bars and brasseries did a roaring trade, a trend partly attributable to the fact that bistro-owners could install tables and chairs on the widened city pavements. But the railways also played a part in contributing to a change of ambience: they brought provincial entrepreneurs and ambitious chefs to the capital, and also inspired a broad spectrum of artists, from Claude Monet to Gustave Caillebotte.

Bistros reflecting France's gastronomic diversity began to open up, offering specialities from regions such as Alsace and Lyons. There has been a traditional *bouillon* (soup kitchen) at 7 rue du Faubourg, Montmartre since 1896, and Pharamond, an 1830s haunt at 24 rue de la Grande Truanderie is known for its *tripes à la mode de Caen* (Caen-style tripe).

Paris was fast becoming a top-flight tourist destination, and successive Expositions Universelles (held in 1867, 1889 and 1900) created a need for hotels. These sprang up in great numbers, and some of the notable ones survive to this day: the Regina on the rue de Rivoli, the Westminster Hotel in rue de la Paix, an example of Second Empire architecture, which took its name from the Duke of Westminster, a regular guest, and the Ritz on the place Vendôme, which opened its revolving doors in 1898.

When Tsar Nicolas II visited the 1900 exhibition and inaugurated the exuberantly Art Nouveau Pont Alexandre III dedicated to his father, there were so many grand dukes in his retinue, milling around the city in search of food and drink, that Parisians invented a phrase that's still used to describe bon vivants doing the rounds of the best restaurants in town: *faire la tournée des grands ducs*.

ABOVE LEFT The Hôtel Regina, on the place des Pyramides, opposite the Louvre, is one of several smart hotels that were opened to accommodate visitors to the Expositions Universelles.

RIGHT AND INSET La Belle Otero (Agustina Otero Iglesias, 1868–1965) and a poster for the Folies Bergère, where she topped the bill.

Courtesans

One of the more intriguing aspects of nineteenth-century popular culture is the aura surrounding the courtesans who took *fin de siècle* Paris by storm. Like the heroine of French naturalist author Emile Zola's Second Empire saga *Nana* (who also featured in an earlier Zola novel, *L 'Assommoir*), these high-flying kept women often started out as ordinary prostitutes. Not all of them destroyed the prosperous gentlemen they preyed upon as Nana did, but many of them became wealthy in their own right, living in stately *hôtels particuliers* given to them by their rich benefactors.

Born in a Spanish fishing port in 1868, Agustina Otero Iglesias (*aka* La Belle Otero) lived to be almost a hundred. Allegedly the cause of several duels and suicides, she had been a *femme fatale* in the true sense of the phrase, becoming one of Europe's most sought-after courtesans. Infamous for her love affairs with dukes, grand dukes and kings, she retired to the Riviera after the First World War, acquiring a mansion said to be worth the equivalent of $15 million today. However, the story goes that her rags-to-riches career went full circle. Once top of the bill at the Folies Bergère, she died penniless.

Double Vision

What is striking about the nineteenth century, to which many French historians refer as a long one, extending from the 1790s to the eve of the First World War, is that it's full of confrontations between direct opposites: neoclassical order versus urban revolts, Napoleonic ostentation versus persistently substandard living conditions, drastic architectural changes versus nostalgia for the Gothic style, fatal cholera epidemics that killed even a prime minister versus Louis Pasteur's health-enhancing discoveries (from pasteurization to his vaccine against rabies). It's impossible to summarize this period in a single snapshot. To do it justice we have to settle for a multi-faceted, 'impressionistic' vision of what amounts to a pivotal century.

Two Parisian must-sees perfectly symbolize the century's contradictory legacy, and I've had the privilege of being treated to an insider's tour of both. There is the triumphalism of the Eiffel Tower, whose chief engineer showed me around his domain with evident pleasure, and there is the site associated with underground, not to say underworld, Paris. I also visited *les égouts de Paris*, our capital's citywide sewage system, devised by the Second Empire engineer Eugène Belgrand. Alongside its technicians, I donned the regulation overall, head torch, gas mask and safety harness to explore their subterranean kingdom. Accessible from the Left Bank side of the Pont de l'Alma, this is Valjean territory – a setting that inevitably evokes the protagonist of Victor Hugo's time-transcending novel *Les Misérables*. In the book the ex-convict Jean Valjean carries Marius to safety after braving the sewers' murky waters. Hugo saw this cavernous labyrinth as the 'conscience of the city', while the photographer Félix Nadar – to whom we owe so many portraits of nineteenth-century luminaries, from Sarah Bernhardt to Edouard Manet – praised it as 'a complete synthesis' of *la vie Parisienne* (Parisian life).

In February 1830, a year before the publication of *Les Misérables*, the first night of Hugo's play *Hernani* had erupted into riots, and thereby crystallized the political and cultural conflicts of the time: romantics versus classicists, liberals versus conformists, republicans versus royalists. Within months of the Trois Glorieuses anti-royalist revolt, Hugo was singled out as the leading light of a politicized brand of liberal Romanticism, designed not only to liberate the arts from the exponents of classicism, but also to free the population from the constraints of the monarchy and despotism in general. Among Hugo's most vociferous 'modernist' supporters were two Romantic poets: Théophile Gautier and Gérard de Nerval.

In the fifteen years preceding his self-exile to Guernsey, after Louis-Napoleon's political takeover, Hugo and his family lived in the Hôtel de Rohan-Guéménée, now a museum, the Maison de Victor Hugo, on the place des Vosges (formerly the place Royale). Gautier had set up house at number 8, and other cultural figures lived near by. Honoré de Balzac's home – also now a museum – was in Passy, at 47 rue Raynouard. At the crossroads of boulevard Raspail and boulevard du Montparnasse is Auguste Rodin's monumental statue of the writer, a powerful tribute to the author of ninety remarkable novels and numerous

short stories. At Balzac's funeral in 1850 Hugo asserted that, 'Henceforth, men's faces will be turned towards the faces not of those who are the rulers but of those who are the thinkers.' He and Gautier were among Balzac's rare intimates, allowed to step into his

sacrosanct study from the garden after uttering a pre-established password – a subterfuge concocted to keep the bailiffs at bay.

Towards the end of the nineteenth century it was painting that was on the agenda, with two competing visions of art – one official, the other independent. The Impressionists broke away from the dictates of the Second Empire's Académie des Beaux-Arts, brushing aside the cobwebs of conventional realism to conjure up vibrantly colourful pictures, more often

ABOVE Auguste Rodin's monumental statue of Balzac was included in an open-air sculpture exhibition in the Champs-Elysées in 1996. Rodin's memorial to the great author caused a scandal when it was first exhibited in 1898.

than not landscapes painted in the open air of their gardens outside Paris. Part of a new wave, these and other non-official artists fashioned a counterculture and succeeded in making their voices heard by mounting exhibitions such as the Salon des Indépendants (independent artists' salon). This was inspired by the Salon des Refusés (Salon of the Rejected), which showed works rejected by the official Salon de Paris. When Napoleon III gave permission for the Refusés show, the intention had been to discredit the artists, who were often noisy in their condemnation of the art establishment, but this exhibition received as much attention as the official one.

Writing about Paul Cézanne in *The Story of Art*, E. H. Gombrich describes how the artist in his youth 'took part in the Impressionist exhibitions, but he was so disgusted by the reception accorded them that he withdrew to his native town of Aix, where he studied the problems of his art, undisturbed by the clamours of the critics'. Nevertheless, Cézanne's Paris years were vital to his subsequent research. It was at the Villa des Arts in the 18th arrondissement that he executed his portrait of the trailblazing art dealer Ambroise Vollard (also painted by Auguste Renoir and Pablo Picasso). Stairway C of this house, later the location of a Fellini film, witnessed an incessant procession of artists, from Paul Signac (a faithful supporter of the pointillist Georges Seurat) to Eugène Carrière (an *intimiste* known for his penetrating portraits of Parisian celebrities, from the statesman Georges Clemenceau to the painter Puvis de Chavannes).

And, of course, there is Montmartre. From the

mid-1850s onwards this artists' village was famed for its cabarets and bohemian lifestyle. The Lapin Agile (Lively Rabbit) at 22 rue des Saules, for example, was owned by a former cancan dancer, whose signature dish was a superb rabbit stew. It was immortalized by the caricaturist André Gill, who emblazoned its sign with a rabbit leaping out of a stewpot, thereby creating a pun – Le Lapin à Gill. Frequented by *fin de siècle* and early twentieth-century authors, such as Marcel Proust, Guillaume Apollinaire and Max Jacob, and hungry artists, including Renoir, Utrillo, Modigliani and Picasso, it has made the leap from one century to the next twice over, and still survives.

Another enduring symbol of Parisian life, the Moulin Rouge, has achieved similar leaps. The place where Toulouse-Lautrec sketched local characters in the heady 1890s went on to host acts by twentieth-century icons, such as Josephine Baker, Mistinguett and Edith Piaf, and then inspired a twenty-first-century feature film starring Nicole Kidman.

A number of artists picked the area of Nouvelle Athènes (New Athens), close to Montmartre, as their base, and added workshops to their houses. Today this leafy 9th arrondissement enclave is blessed with two museums within walking distance of the place Saint-Georges. The Musée Gustave Moreau at 14 rue de la Rochefoucauld is an opulent, Empire-decorated abode that the artist himself bequeathed to the state. It includes a shrine-like boudoir dedicated to the memory of his only known mistress, Alexandrine, who died at the age of fifty-four. The Musée de l'Art Romantique (Museum of Romantic Art) in the Hôtel

ABOVE Josephine Baker (1906–75) just being herself – her recipe for conquering *le tout-Paris* (all of Paris) at the beginning of the twentieth century.

Scheffer-Renan on rue Chaptal was once the home of Ary Scheffer, an artist whose cultural salons were the talk of the town in the 1850s. In his Restoration-style living room, *tout* Paris mingled with his writer and composer friends, who included George Sand, Frédéric Chopin, Franz Liszt, Ivan Turgenev and Charles Dickens.

Music and theatre also went through many changes and developments, and Parisians enjoyed a wide variety of entertainments throughout the nineteenth century. Street theatre, fairground acts, cabaret shows, operettas, tragedies … Of course, they didn't necessarily all appeal to the same audiences, and some pushed the boundaries of acceptability just a bit too far. Igor Stravinsky's *The Rite of Spring*, for example, premièred at the Théâtre des Champs-Élysées in 1913, caused a great scandal because of its daring costumes, strange choreography and shocking plot that included pagan sacrifice.

The nineteenth century was a complex era, and as I wander through the Louvre's rooms, studying the works from that time, it seems impossible to select one painting that represents it more accurately than any other. If David's depiction of the crowning of Napoleon I is set aside as being emblematic of Bonaparte's imperial dream rather than representative of an entire century's dualities, it doesn't take long to narrow the choice down to a couple of serious contenders: Delacroix's *La Liberté guidant le peuple*, (Liberty Leading the People) painted not as a tribute to the Revolution of 1789, as visitors to the museum tend to assume, but to commemorate the Trois Glorieuses

of the July Revolution in 1830. Or how about Théodore Géricault's *La Radeau de la Méduse* (The Raft of the Medusa)? Back in 1819, this monumental composition triggered a national scandal. Why? Because it depicted the dramatic consequences of an event that had actually, and recently, taken place: the captain of a wrecked ship had left his crew and passengers to die. Enthralled by its spectacular *mise-en-scène*, Delacroix posed for one of the dying figures hanging on to the makeshift raft. It is as if Géricault had foreseen the life or death existential dilemmas that would come into play as the curtain fell on the nineteenth century. Two centuries on, it remains mesmerizing.

At the turn of that century Parisians were in a collective quandary, literally not knowing what to cling to. Was it better to look the grim realities of the Industrial Age in the face, as Hugo, Balzac, Stendhal and Zola had done? Or should they take refuge in Symbolist mysticism? Was there an antidote to this *mal du siècle* (sickness of the century)? Such were the questions that perplexed café society at the time.

What was the best remedy for the feeling of listlessness that overwhelmed sensitive souls at the dawn of the twentieth century? Should they take a walk down memory lane in the tracks of Marcel Proust? And, if so, how far back should they go? Should they return to their ancestors, 'nos ancêtres les Gaulois', as Jules Michelet had put it in his nineteen-volume history of France, completed in 1867? Now excluded from school textbooks, this momentous phrase had kindled renewed interest in Gallic lore. The Middle Ages were in fashion. After being placed in charge of the restoration of

ABOVE *Musique aux Tuileries*
(Music in the Tuileries), 1862.
Famous for his *Le déjeuner sur
l'herbe* (*Luncheon on the Grass*),
Edouard Manet included a self-
portrait and also depicted many
of his friends – artists, authors
and musicians – in this early
work, which captures the carefree
atmosphere of the Tuileries
Gardens as he knew it.

Notre-Dame, Eugène Viollet-le-Duc had become the
high priest of neo-Gothic architecture, commissioned
to redo private homes in his intricate style.

Was there a hint of narcissism in so much intro-
spection? Perhaps. After all, many of the languorous
flâneurs who promenaded from one part of the capital
to another had acquired a habit that would inevitably
alter their perceptions: they were increasingly accustomed to seeing their way of life through the prism of
photography and film. Whatever they did next would
be recorded by photographers and film-makers, so
they'd better watch their step.

PARIS REINVENTED

Why not admit it? Paris is a museum. But what a museum! It's a surprisingly well-balanced city, a mixture of classicism, innovation and avant-garde experimentation.

From painting to literature, music to architecture, fashion to cinema, twentieth-century Parisian style-setters have always been 'in tune' with their time. Neither two world wars, nor a succession of colonial conflicts, nor some memorable home-grown protests have cramped the creativity of Paris. Indeed, adversity has often fed it. The ability to sense what is 'in the air' at a given moment is a gift that's often attributed to Paris-based artists and couturiers, from wherever they hail. For good reason our City of Light (and leading lights) is also designated the 'Capital of Style'.

It has been suggested that when Paris lost its crown to New York as the capital of modern art in the first half of the century, it also lost its edge, and has since gone through something of an identity crisis. I think it would be more accurate to describe it as going through a period of chop and change, making vital contributions to distinct disciplines at various points in time. Nonetheless, Paris is currently at the heart of a classic philosophical question, torn between *l'être*

(being) and *le paraître* (appearing). On the one hand it is France's rigorously planned Haussmannian capital, and on the other it is a multi-cultural mosaic in the process of redefining itself.

If asked to name a symbol of Paris, most sight-seers would nominate the Eiffel Tower. Yet another, less well-known metallic construction, built for the 1900 Exposition Universelle, seems more representative of the contradictions underlying the city's ongoing metamorphosis. This alternative icon is the Grand Palais, the place where the 'wild' brushstrokes and colours of Henri Matisse and his Fauvist friends caused such a stir at the 1905 Salon d'Automne that a critic heatedly described their room as a 'cage aux fauves' (cage of wild animals). Little did he imagine that he was coining the name of what would become an eminent modern-art movement.

Since its recent restoration, the Grand Palais has again become a pillar of the city's arts-and-style scene, hosting everything from fine-art exhibitions and haute-couture extravaganzas to performances of rap

music. This has led to yet another question: should street artists from the *banlieues* take part in state-initiated projects of this nature, or are they becoming part of the establishment if they do? This is exactly the kind of issue that reflects the present mood of Paris.

Most French people would deny that culture is a commodity like any other, even though corporate sponsorship of cultural events is commonplace, and no longer viewed with disdain by museums and other 'serious' institutions. Since the first Ministry of Culture was established in 1959, French governments have been committed to nurturing the arts. In 1982 Jack Lang, the then minister of culture, launched the Fête de la Musique, a massive all-night celebration of music in its many forms, held on 21 June, the first day of summer. As further evidence of the special relationship between state and culture there is an unemployment insurance scheme for members of the acting profession and entertainment industry. However, this 'alliance' coexists with a tradition of artistic independence, as epitomized by the nineteenth-century artists who refused to participate in official exhibitions and instead founded the Salon des Indépendants (see page 142).

In this spirit a new tradition has gained ground. Our principal art fairs and performing-arts festivals now have unofficial 'Off' editions (rather like off-Broadway shows), which aim to promote emerging artists. These include 'Show Off' during the official FIAC (International Contemporary Art Fair), and the 'Mois de la Photo Off', which coincides with the 'Mois de la Photo' biennial photography show.

Metropolitan Culture

There's no denying that art and style are incredibly important in Paris, and sometimes it has been difficult to accommodate both in pursuit of progress. During the final decade of the nineteenth century a major debate was raging in Paris. How could this city, supposedly the civilized capital of the world, still not have a metro system? Both London and New York had begun theirs in the 1860s, but Paris had spent three decades debating what form its metro should take. The most favoured solution was an elevated system, as in New York. The alternative, a London-style underground, was considered inappropriate for Parisians, whom city planners believed were 'avid for liberty, for air, for light'. Travelling underground, it was argued, would destroy the city's *flâneur* culture and consequently all the merchants and tradesmen who depended on the 'promenading instinct' of their clientele. More vociferous detractors claimed 'there will no longer be a Paris'.

These negative voices were eventually silenced and the city embarked on building an underground system. After the first line opened in July 1900, millions of passengers flocked to use it, and rapidly came to perceive it as an essential part of everyday life. Parisians didn't 'refuse' the Métro, nor did they cease to be *flâneurs*. The city survived, indeed flourished, and the Paris Métro is now considered a model of its kind.

Hector Guimard's Art Nouveau underground entrances are familiar to fans of our capital all over the world. Their Métropolitain logo is all that remains of

The events of May '68

Even to Parisians born after 1968, the wave of student and worker protests referred to as *les événements de Mai 68* (the events of May '68) or simply Mai 68 has acquired a mythical dimension. Although the veterans of its legendary demonstrations, known as *soixante-huitards* (the sixty-eighters), are sometimes mentioned in conversation with a touch of irony, there is a lot of respect for the changes they obtained, for instance in terms women's liberation.

De Gaulle was re-elected in June 1968. However, he finally retired as president following the defeat of his April 1969 referendum. On the opposite side of the barricades, another icon had entered history: Daniel Cohn-Bendit – dubbed 'Danny the red' because of his politics and the colour of his hair – became the voice of a generation: *la génération de 68*. Cohn-Bendit is now a prominent figure of the environmental-protest movement (co-President of the EU's European Greens–European Free Alliance group). So, newspapers occasionally call him 'Danny the green'.

Graffiti and posters popped up all over Paris during May '68. The most famous – like the one featuring the slogan *Sois jeune et tais toi* (Be Young and Shut Up) with a silhouette of General de Gaulle – are now collector's items.

the original name of the Paris Métro system, which came into being just in time for the 1900 Exposition Universelle. As visitors to the city soon notice, this is not the only connection between our sixteen-line rapid-transit system and the arts. In recent years many contemporary artists have been commissioned to revamp its stations. A notable example is Louvre-Palais-Royal, decorated with coloured-glass balls by Jean-Michel Othoniel. This happens to be the stop for Paris's famous *Colonnes de Buren* sculpture, situated in the great courtyard of the Palais Royal, where the Ministry of Culture is located. Initially controversial, this 3000-square metre (11,000-square foot) sculpture, composed of black-and-white striped columns of varying heights, has come to be considered a fully fledged Parisian landmark. Officially described as 'conceptual' or 'minimalist', it is rarely referred to by its real name, *Les deux plateaux*. The artist behind this monumental installation is Daniel Buren, a precursor of 'street art'. He started out in the late 1960s by producing 'unofficial' public artworks using the striped awning fabric in general use in France, and this gradually became his 'signature'.

The names of numerous Métro stations are linked to key historical events, such as République and Quatre-Septembre. Several on Line 1 (the first to be inaugurated) pay tribute to major twentieth-century figures, such as Charles de Gaulle, France's ultimate political hero, the US president Franklin D. Roosevelt, and the British sovereign George V. Also commemorated are the First World War statesman Georges Clemenceau (Lines 1 and 13) and the author Emile Zola (Line 10),

RIGHT The Stade de France sports stadium was built for the football World Cup in 1998. It also hosts all kinds of large-scale entertainment projects and is used as a venue for rock concerts featuring crowd-drawing bands, from the Rolling Stones to U2. In September 2006 it became an arena in the gladiatorial sense, hosting a *Ben Hur* musical produced by the French actor and film director Robert Hossein.

the two figures most responsible for ensuring a happy ending to the Dreyfus Affair (see page 106).

Certain stops are more poignant than others. During the course of the First World War the Gare de l'Est was the point of departure for soldiers dispatched to the Eastern Front, where a whole generation of young men was killed or mutilated. Others are dedicated to the memory of Second World War *résistants*, such as 'Colonel Fabien' (Pierre George) and Charles Michels, and civilians shot during the German Occupation, including Jacques Bonsergent (the first Parisian to be killed) and Corentin Cariou (a hostage). Métro Stalingrad evokes a turning point in the war, remembered as the bloodiest battle in human history.

On the Left Bank several stations remind Parisians of May '68, when student strikes turned into street battles and France changed forever. Métro Odéon, for example, is the stop for the Théâtre de l'Odéon, where the directors of the theatre, Jean-Louis Barrault and Madeleine Renault, allowed students to occupy the premises. Unfortunately, considerable damage was done to technical equipment, and valuable old costumes were burnt. André Malraux, the then minister of culture, blamed the couple for letting the situation get out of hand and fired them. They went on to 'do their own thing' at the Gare d'Orsay (a nineteenth-century railway station later converted into a museum by Italian architect Gae Aulenti) and at the Théâtre du Rond-Point on the Champs-Elysées.

A lot of Métro stops allude to places or events that convey little or nothing to Parisians nowadays. In the multi-ethnic Goutte d'Or neighbourhood of northeast Paris, named after the 'golden' white wine produced there until the end of the nineteenth century, Métro Château Rouge owes its name to a public ballroom frequented by revolutionaries in 1848. Part of a mansion formerly used as command post by Napoleon Bonaparte, this handsome red-brick establishment was closed in 1882 and subsequently demolished.

Others stops are a nod in the direction of the arts. Bobigny-Pablo Picasso pays tribute to the city's most famous adopted son, while Bobigny-Pantin Raymond Queneau commemorates the Surrealist poet and mathematician who also wrote the best-selling novel *Zazie dans le Métro* (1959), famously adapted for the screen by the director Louis Malle.

Historically bounded by city walls, Paris is now encircled by roads, Métro lines, bus routes and the T3 tramway system. Indeed, the Périphérique, a two-way ring road, functions much like a feudal wall. It hems in Paris's citizens, creating a demarcation line beyond which taxi fares increase, but it also enables motorists to whizz from one *porte* (city gate) to the next, or one *quartier* to another, without crossing the centre. Should they want to cross town, the futuristic conductorless Météor line whisks them over in a matter of minutes. Alternatively, they can hop on the recently constructed T3 system, also known as the Tramway des Maréchaux because it runs along boulevards bearing the names of Napoleonic marshals.

Areas inside and outside the 'wall' of the Périphérique are connected by road and rail. The Réseau Express Régionale (RER), a network of express trains, links the capital to the *petite couronne* (little crown) formed by three immediately adjacent *départements* (the Hauts-de-Seine, Seine-Saint-Denis and Val-de-Marne), and to the outer suburbs of the *grande couronne* (big crown). In addition, Line 13 of the Métro was extended all the way to the Saint-Denis soccer stadium, built for the World Cup in 1998.

Boho Spirit

In 1965 the singer Charles Aznavour enjoyed a huge hit with 'La Bohème', a tribute to the live and let-live attitude that has drawn so many people to Paris. In the build-up to the year 2000 celebrations marketing analysts highlighted a new type of bohemian, a 'nomadic spirit' more likely to be riding the Métro

ABOVE Singer Charles Aznavour enjoyed a huge hit with 'La Bohème', a nostalgic tribute to his bohemian youth.
OPPOSITE Catherine Demongeot starred as the epnoymous heroine of *Zazie dans le Métro* (1960), Louis Malle's film comedy with a zany storyline. A petulant twelve-year-old obliged to spend two days with relatives in Paris explores the Métro.

Shakespeare and Company

Sylvia Beach was just another American student in Paris when she pushed open the door of the Maison des Amis des Livres, a bookshop owned by Adrienne Monnier, one of the first women in France to establish herself as an independent bookseller. Upon leaving it, however, Beach was quite a different person, for she had met the kindred spirit who inspired her to open her own bookshop, which she called Shakespeare and Company.

Beach's chief claim to fame is being the first to publish James Joyce's *Ulysses* (in 1922). Sadly, that didn't deter the renowned Irish writer from moving to another publisher and leaving her in financial difficulties. Fortunately, André Gide flew to her rescue, persuading fellow authors to subscribe to a 'Friends' club.

Sylvia Beach eventually gave permission for a shop of the same name to be opened by George Whitman at 37 rue de la Bûcherie, and it became a haven for writers of the beat generation, such as Allen Ginsberg and William Burroughs. Registered as a historical monument by the Ministry of Culture, this 'wonderland of books', as Henry Miller once called it, is now run by Sylvia Beach Whitman, the daughter of George, whom he named after the woman he so admired.

OPPOSITE George Whitman once described his bookshop opposite Notre-Dame Cathedral as akin to 'a never ending play by William Shakespeare, where the Romeos and Juliets are forever young while I have become an octogenarian … like King Lear.'

RIGHT Sylvia Beach in the original Shakespeare and Company and (**TOP**) in the shop doorway with the Irish writer James Joyce.

with backpack and mobile phone than eking out an existence in a garret. A series of prolonged strikes revealed that these new-style Parisians continued to travel to work and explore the city by other means if deprived of public transport – cycling or skating to and from their destinations in an eco-friendly way. As it turned out, a good many of these 'nouveaux nomads' were also 'bobos' – 'bourgeois-bohemian' consumers who tend to live in the capital's increas-ingly gentrified *quartiers populaires* (see page 13).

There are still vestiges of the original, nine-teenth-century bohemian lifestyle for which Paris is famed, and which was beautifully conveyed in Arthur Rimbaud's famous poem 'Ma Bohème'. Indeed, year after year students embarking on a 'grand tour' of Europe visit the cafés in Saint-Germain-des-Prés and Montparnasse where celebrated artists and authors once gathered. At the Père-Lachaise cemetery they

ABOVE Among the graves of many famous figures whose final resting place is the Père-Lachaise cemetery, there is that of French music icon Serge Gainsbourg, whose hits include 'Dieu fumeur de Havanes' (God is a smoker of Havanas).

The misty alleys of the Père-Lachaise cemetery resonate with the verse and lyrics of the many illustrious poets and artists buried in its midst.

search out a latter-day bohemian, Jim Morrison, the lead singer with The Doors, who died mysteriously in Parisian lodgings, and is said to have described himself as 'a Rimbaud with a leather jacket'.

Another icon who drew inspiration from Rimbaud was the American author Henry Miller, who lived in Paris for a number of years and produced a study of the writer. However, the quintessential American in Paris was undoubtedly Ernest Hemingway. A notable 1920s expatriate, he, and others like him, were attracted to the comparatively cosmopolitan atmosphere of the city's bohemian quarters, and loved to visit

Shakespeare and Company, a gipsy caravan of a store, laden with new, used and antiquarian books. The American writer Gertrude Stein became Hemingway's mentor in Paris, and introduced him to members of the Modern Movement, who had picked Montparnasse as their base. This is where he wrote his cult 'Lost Generation' novel, *The Sun Also Rises* (1926), at his favourite restaurant, La Closeries des Lilas.

Paris has long been considered one of those places that provokes a sense of *dépaysement* – a feeling of being 'somewhere different', where you can 'make a difference'. It was this feeling that attracted creative

OPPOSITE LEFT Henry Miller based his novel *Quiet Days in Clichy* (1956) on his real-life experiences as a young author living in cheap, furnished accommodation in Paris's red-light district.

OPPOSITE RIGHT Ernest Hemingway also published a first-hand account of his life in Paris. Although it was set in the 1920s, his celebrated journal

A Moveable Feast contains the addresses of cafés, bars and hotels that can still be found in modern-day Paris.

ABOVE LEFT Hemingway's mentor, Gertrude Stein, spent most of her life in France.

ABOVE RIGHT The writer F. Scott Fitzgerald and his wife, Zelda, lived in Paris in the mid-1920s and featured in *A Moveable Feast*, along with Joyce and Stein.

types like Hemingway, and kept them coming back for more. It allowed them to invent, or reinvent, in ways that they couldn't 'back home'. What better place for Hemingway to develop his direct narrative style than in the city he recalled as a 'moveable feast'? Perhaps he was thinking of the pigeons he'd shot in the Luxembourg Gardens in order to feed himself while still a struggling unknown. Or perhaps he was thinking of the bar at the Ritz, which he claimed to have 'personally liberated' in 1944, and which was subsequently renamed the 'Hemingway Bar'.

During the 1890s, the 'capital of Bohemia' was

Montmartre, where the anarchistic spirit of the 1870 uprising lingered. Here was the Bateau Lavoir, the studio where Picasso unveiled his revolutionary *Demoiselles d'Avignon* painting to fellow hungry artists such as Amedeo Modigliani and Henri Rousseau, and the poets Guillaume Apollinaire and Max Jacob. Destroyed by fire in 1970, this cultural landmark was rebuilt by the architect Claude Charpentier and currently houses foreign artists in residence.

Historically, artists and writers have always been drawn to relatively 'picturesque' bastions of Parisian popular culture offering low rents. The cycle is always the same: as soon as the area they like starts to become gentrified, and therefore too expensive and less inspirational, they're obliged to decamp. Thus did Montmartre give way to Montparnasse. The atmosphere of this quarter's heyday lives on at the Musée du Montparnasse, nestled in a leafy, cobblestoned courtyard at 21 avenue du Maine. This congenial museum is housed in the studio of Marie Vassilieff, the founder of Paris's Russian Academy. She was the 'heart and soul' of the neighbourhood's bohemian community, offering a creative atmosphere that benefited many notable artists, including Henri Matisse, Marc Chagall and Fernand Léger, and the composer Erik Satie. She is also fondly remembered for the 'canteen' she created for undernourished artists during the First World War. In 1927 she applied her own talent to ornamental panels displayed on pillars at La Coupole brasserie, where the memoirs of another 'pillar' of local bohemia – Kiki de Montparnasse (real name Alice Prin) – were launched two years later. Thanks to their explicit content, these recollections of Montparnasse life were banned in the United States until the 1970s.

What is left of Montparnasse's bohemian spirit? The boulevard du Montparnasse brasseries (La Coupole, La Rotonde, Le Dôme, Le Sélect) that used to be favoured haunts of such living legends as Hemingway and Picasso, continue to be patronized by a curious cocktail of tourists and distinctly 'upmarket' artists. La Coupole, however, has attempted to 'maintain the flame' by hosting salsa and 'slam' (instant urban-poetry) sessions.

Not open to the public, but worth looking at from the exterior, La Ruche (in passage de Dantzig) is an additional boho site with history. Designed by Gustave Eiffel for use as a wine rotunda at the Exposition Universelle of 1900, it was then dismantled and rebuilt by Alfred Boucher as a three-storey artists' 'village'. The word *ruche* means 'beehive', a reference to the building's strange shape, but it's also true to say that at one point it was a hive of creative energy, sheltering penniless geniuses – all *habitués* of Marie Vassilieff's kitchen – whose work would one day be worth its weight in gold. When it was threatened with demolition by greedy developers in the 1960s, the building was saved by a group of luminaries that included Jean-Paul Sartre and Jean Renoir, and its lucky tenants were able to celebrate its centenary in 2003.

Modern art's heroic bohemian era is looked back upon with nostalgia by those who imagine its figureheads painting their masterpieces in cool 'bobo-style' lofts, like those in present-day Montmartre or

ABOVE La Coupole, along with La Rotonde, Le Dôme and Le Sélect, is one of Montparnasse's renowned brasseries.

OVERLEAF Many of the boulevard Saint-Germain's cafés, including Les Deux Magots, became Left Bank landmarks, associated with famous artists, writers, musicians and film-makers.

Once the daily haunts of Hemingway and Picasso, the brasseries on the boulevard de Montparnasse continue to attract a curious cocktail of tourists and distinctly 'upmarket' artists.

OPPOSITE Juliette Greco, the muse of post-Second-World-War Saint-Germain-des-Prés, 'the birthplace of Existentialism'. Even Jean-Paul Sartre wrote lyrics for the singer–actress, whose legendary existence includes a romance with Miles Davis.

ABOVE LEFT The Existentialist writer and philosopher Jean-Paul Sartre in 1964, the year he declined the Nobel Prize for literature.

ABOVE RIGHT Simone de Beauvoir, the author of *The Second Sex*. Saint-Germain-des-Prés was Sartre and Beauvoir territory until a new wave of stylish fashion boutiques stepped in.

Montparnasse. In fact, few artists can afford to live in central Paris any more as prices have soared. As a general rule, Parisian landlords will rent living or working space only to tenants who can prove that they have a stable, salaried position and earn the equivalent of three times the rent requested. In order to help creative types, the French government makes an *exception culturelle*, and provides a special social-benefits system administrated by La Maison des Artistes (House of Artists). It also offers state-subsidized studios integrated in HLM buildings (see page 16), usually on the outskirts of the city. Unfortunately, there is a long,

long waiting list for these places, and fewer of them are being built than in the past. As a result, artists' squats have been springing up in various parts of the capital.

The boho streets where the singer Juliette Greco used to wander along in her lovers' overcoats have changed in ways that are sad but, it seems, inevitable. Old-established booksellers and art galleries around Saint-Germain-des-Prés protested that they were being 'colonized' by chic fashion brands, which were gradually buying up their premises. Opposite the Café de Flore and Les Deux Magots, smoky venues where Jean-Paul Sartre and his contemporaries discussed Existentialism, Emporio Armani has set up shop – in this case a suave boutique and café overlooking the Carrefour Saint-Germain.

Where have all the Left Bank galleries gone? Those with strong historical links to Saint-Germain (Galerie La Hune, Galerie Claude Bernard and Galerie Jeanne-

ABOVE Parisians often refer to the Pompidou Centre as 'Beaubourg' – meaning *beau* (beautiful) and *bourg* (small town or borough). When it opened in 1977, critics of the museum's innovative architecture described it as an oil refinery, destroying the cachet of Paris's historical Marais quarter.

Bucher, for example) have stuck to their guns. Others have 'capitulated' and moved on. In the 1980s, when Jack Lang was minister of culture, many offbeat art spaces flourished in and around the Bastille. Successful artists and collectors of their work flocked to the area, converting its traditional craftsmen's workshops into New York-style lofts. Boosted by the presence of its modern opera house, it has since become one of Paris-by-night's most crowded neighbourhoods, with more restaurants, clubs and music venues than art galleries.

At the moment, many galleries are moving to the Haut Marais, an upmarket area of the Marais that's been 'invaded' by a new wave of bobos. On Saturday afternoons cool art lovers stroll around Beaubourg, visiting the latest exhibitions to be seen at the Pompidou Centre and in the streets adjacent to the museum. Their next stop is the rue Louise Weiss, in the 13th arrondissement, a few Métro stations away from the Bibliothèque Nationale (National Library), where a group of state-subsidized galleries show mainstream and experimental artists.

Just as artistic locales are constantly changing, so is art itself. Where Cubism began, and Fauvists, Dadaists and Surrealists once flourished, a new generation of artists experiments and gains inspiration from the city.

New Waves

If France was the capital of the art world at the onset of the twentieth century, by the second half that distinction had shifted to New York, where a new wave of 'action' painters and Abstract Expressionists had started to produce large-scale canvases. Meanwhile, Paris was generating a new wave of independent filmmakers, who used non-professional actors and shot outdoors. Their films broke away from the dictates of classical cinematic form, showing Paris in a new light. Several of these directors, described as *auteurs* (authors) because their work had a 'personal signature', had started out as critics for *Cahiers du Cinéma*,

RIGHT Paris's national library, the Bibliothèque Nationale de France, boasts two main sites: the new Site François-Mitterrand in the 13th arrondissement and the historical Site Richelieu. The architectural highlights of the latter include seventeenth-century buildings by Sun King protégé François Mansart and the awe-inspiring oval library (pictured here), which was inaugurated in 1936.

Paris on camera

From the Eiffel Tower to the Métro, which featured in *Zazie dans le Métro* (1960) and *Subway* (1985), certain Parisian locations are film stars in their own right. Sometimes it's hard to separate the magic of Paris from *la magie du cinéma*.

A masterpiece of Poetic Realism filmed during the Nazi occupation, Marcel Carné's *Les Enfants du Paradis* (Children of Paradise), re-creates the atmosphere of the capital in the early nineteenth century, before Baron Haussmann reconstructed it.

In 1991, Léos Carax planned to give the Pont Neuf, the oldest bridge in Paris, a starring role in *Les Amants du Pont-Neuf*, but scheduling difficulties obliged him to abandon location shooting and to build a replica of it in the Camargue region. The film's magic ingredient? A spectacular jet-ski sequence.

Instead of concentrating on the city's cinegenic landmarks, a new New Wave of fast-paced modern movies is attuned to the pulse of present-day Paris. *Ne le dis à personne* (Tell no one),

Guillaume Canet's adaptation of Harlan Coben's thriller, is even more 'breathless' than Jean-Luc Godard's cult 1960 detective story *A Bout de Souffle* (Breathless).

Key movies set in Paris. **ABOVE LEFT** *Les Amants du Pont-Neuf* (1991). **ABOVE** Christophe Lambert in *Subway* (1985). **RIGHT** Jean-Paul Belmondo and Jean Seberg in *A bout de souffle* (Breathless).

the most influential film magazine at that time. Both François Truffaut's *Les Quatre Cent Coups* (The 400 Blows, 1959) and Jean-Luc Godard's *A Bout de Souffle* (Breathless, 1960) were internationally acclaimed. Hectic 'jump-cuts' and hand-held camera sequences gave street scenes, such as those in Godard's *Weekend*, an unprecedented feeling of mobility – something that this millennium's phone-cam users take for granted.

The advent of photography and moving pictures in the second half of the nineteenth century sharpened the curiosity of *flâneurs*, prompting them to visit parts of the city with which they were unfamiliar. This 'nomadic' approach to Parisian life has been given a fresh twist via a couple of widely publicized annual events initiated by the City of Paris in the 2000s. The first is 'Nuit Blanche' (White Night), a weekend in

ABOVE French cinema's New Wave directors filmed real-life situations in real-time, in this case a scene from Jean-Luc Godard's 1964 film noir, *Bande à part* (The Outsiders).

October, when the public can view outdoor installations by experimental artists and film-makers throughout the night. Another installation that gets Parisians on the move is the artificial beach named Paris-Plage that is set up on the banks of the Seine in the summer months. Complete with palm trees, parasols and Riviera-style recliners, it gives city dwellers a touch of the Mediterranean.

Film has a special place in the hearts of Parisians, sometimes for reasons not connected with movies themselves. Darkened cinemas offer protection from cold and prying eyes, which during the war years made them an ideal rendezvous for members of the Resistance to exchange information. Of course, they continue to be a favourite meeting place for lovers, something else for which Paris has an unparalleled reputation. Less retiring individuals can visit the Parc de la Villette, which hosts an open-air cinema festival in the summer. Here you can hire a deck chair and blanket for the evening to view films on a giant screen.

Nowadays, thanks to another government-sponsored *exception culturelle*, those keen on film can indulge in a spot of further education at the capital's *cinémas d'art et d'essai*. These specialize in *films d'auteurs* and vintage movies, encouraging Parisians to 'revisit' their classics. L'Epée de Bois (The Wooden Sword) is a charming example on the rue Mouffetard, while Le Balzac is the last privately owned cinema on the Champs-Elysées. Both also occasionally show the work of young artists on their walls.

Paris's newest pantheon for film buffs is the Cinémathèque in Bercy, a post-modern edifice

CLOCKWISE FROM TOP LEFT
Fashion designers Coco Chanel, Christian Dior, Yves Saint Laurent and Karl Lagerfeld, and the multi-talented writer, poet, film-maker and artist Jean Cocteau – all of them Paris-based creative spirits who had the ability to sense what is 'in the air'.

designed by the American architect Frank Gehry. It has four state-of-the-art screening rooms, and a museum that contains an impressive collection of documents and memorabilia connected with cinema. Among these is the dress that Vivien Leigh wore in *Gone with the Wind* (1939). Of course, this is not the 'original version' of the cinema archive envisioned by Henri Langlois in 1936. It has been housed in several locations over the years, the last of which was the Palais de Chaillot on the place du Trocadéro.

Next door to the Rex Club, the HQ for electro *soirées* hosted by French Touch DJ Laurent Garnier, stands a cinematic monument: the Grand Rex. One of our city's oldest *grand-boulevard* cinemas, it offers behind-the-scenes tours of its baroquely spectacular Art Deco premises.

Fashion Focus

Few would contest Paris's claim to being the capital of couture. The Triangle d'Or (Golden Triangle) in the 8th arrondissement is home to all the major couture houses, but how did this come about?

Various factors influenced fashion at the beginning of the twentieth century, blurring the boundaries between masculine and feminine attire. The wider use of bicycles and cars, then still fairly new inventions, played a part, and the two world wars also had decisive, practical consequences. In fact, considered overall, twentieth-century fashion is marked by a series of 'liberations', beginning with liberation from the corset by Paul Poiret in the wake of the First World War. In the 1920s and 1930s Elsa Schiaparelli took Paris by storm with her Surrealist creations, including

ABOVE, LEFT TO RIGHT

'Liberated' mid-1960s
creations by Federico Forquet,
Emilio Pucci, Paco Rabanne and
Rudi Gernreich. From Sonia
Delaunay's colourful fabrics to
op' (optical) and pop art, the
visual arts have always inspired
Parisian couturiers.

a 'telephone bag', and various hat and jewellery collaborations with the Surrealist artist Salvador Dali and the theatre director Jean Cocteau.

During the 1930s came *garçonnes* – boyish girls sporting short skirts and bobbed haircuts. The chief exponent of menswear-inspired fashion was Coco Chanel, who had a knack for transforming fundamental social changes into era-defining styles. At her salon she created a wide range of streetwise-yet-chic clothing that became her signature. One of her greatest achievements was to take the stiffness out of women's suits, giving them the same freedom of movement that men expect from their clothes, but never losing their femininity. Although the much copied Chanel suit was eventually dismissed as an outmoded symbol representing 'the discreet charm of the

ABOVE Gaultier for ever.
France's coolest couturier,
Jean Paul Gaultier, describes
the creative process with
typically Parisian gesticulation.

bourgeoisie', it was later given new life when Karl Lagerfeld joined the House of Chanel and updated it.

Generations of women are thankful for Chanel's creation of the 'little black dress', or LBD as it has become known. She advocated it as a basic item in every modern woman's wardrobe, and there are few who don't heed her advice. She understood the demands that everyday life placed on women, and dressed them for both comfort and style. Lagerfeld, her successor, follows the same principles. He doesn't hesitate to borrow from, say, hip-hop culture, bringing a touch of urban attitude to his interpretation of the Chanel spirit.

Shortly after Charles de Gaulle made his historic speech announcing the liberation of Paris in August 1944, Christian Dior launched his elegant New Look, characterized by wasp-waisted full skirts, liberating his stylish clientele from the dowdy attire imposed by the economic constraints of the Second World War. Soon resourceful Parisiennes and their dressmakers were copying the look, and women around the world were rediscovering the pleasure of truly feminine attire.

During the Swinging '60s style exploded in a variety of directions, in a spirit of 'anything goes'. Once again, women were liberated – this time from fashion's rules and regulations. Yves Saint Laurent decided that it was OK for women to wear dinner jackets, so he designed innumerable versions of his trademark, *le smoking*. Back in 1911, Sonia Delaunay designed colourful fabrics with circular motifs. Similarly, in the 1960s, op art found its way on to mini dresses, as did the geometric designs seen in paintings by Piet Mondrian. The dialogue between art and high fashion was never livelier.

In the countdown to May '68, liberation from 'down to earth' bourgeois values was in the air and Parisian fashion reflected this. French couturiers, such as Emanuel Ungaro, Pierre Cardin and André Courrèges, conceived Space Age clothes and accessories, expressing a vision of the future that now seems quaintly out of date. Still, it's a lot of fun to look back at their ideas, not least Paco Rabane's plastic and metal 'chainmail' dresses that had to be worn without tights because the dresses ripped them to shreds.

What's become of the avant-garde in fashion? Should we seek it at catwalk shows held at the Carrousel du Louvre or Grand Palais, or should we head for the rue des Gardes (a street situated in the Goutte d'Or, where young designers can rent state-subsidized boutiques, fashion's equivalent of the rue Louise Weiss)? One option is to refuse to choose between past, present and future. Jean Paul Gaultier recently decided to present a thirty-year retrospective of his 'landmark' styles, which include striped sailor sweaters, skirts for men, tutus twinned with leather jackets and pointy bras. Instead of showing a straightforward seasonal collection, he proved that he has been consistently avant-garde over the years. Like Elsa Schiaparelli's hats, Gaultier's past inventions were ahead of their time and still strike us as incredibly original.

At the helm of a brand called Resistance, alternative fashion designer Ramdane Touhami remains truest to the military meaning of 'avant-garde' — a

ABOVE Madonna sporting an unmistakably Gaultier creation on her *Blond Ambition* tour in Japan in 1990.

Flea Markets

The fad for Art Deco furniture and vintage clothing has given Paris's *marchés aux puces* (flea markets) a new lease of life. The colloquial expression for rummaging through stallholders' wares in search of antiques or second-hand bargains is *chiner*, and Parisians who indulge in this pastime are called *chineurs*. There's even a chic restaurant in the Haut-Marais called Les Chineurs.

On Saturday and Sunday, head for the Puces de Vanves on the capital's southern periphery, or the Puces de Saint-Ouen (which is also open on Monday) just north of Paris (take the Métro to Porte de Clignancourt). Saint-Ouen boasts a series of 'mini-markets'. The oldest is the Marché Vernaison at 99 rue des Rosiers, while the Marché Paul Bert, on the corner of the rue des Rosiers and rue Paul Bert, appeared after the Second World War. Although not quite as chic as the Marché Biron (at 85 rue des Rosiers), it's said to be the best.

soldier sent out to assess the ground ahead of his companions. In his barrack-like shop he sells clothes that express a militant viewpoint about fashion and society, such as combat jackets emblazoned with cautionary anti-consumerist messages.

A Living Museum?

Paris has sometimes been accused of being a living museum resting on its artistic and architectural laurels, unable to remain the Capital of Style without calling for 'outside reinforcements'. Accusers point to the likes of John Galliano, Marc Jacobs and Alexander McQueen, two Englishmen and an American, who were invited to revive the ailing fashion houses of Dior, Louis Vuitton and Givenchy respectively. Is this accusation accurate, or is the city simply working its magic and attracting the best in their fields to rise to even greater heights?

To a certain extent, it's true that the French sometimes seem unenthusiastic about new ideas. We have critical minds and we like to exercise them, so what better target than the latest innovation? Some would claim that this combative attitude simply proves people care. What is certainly true is that, despite the ongoing battle between advocates of classicism and innovation, experimentation and reason, Paris is a surprisingly well-balanced city.

Why not admit it? Paris is a museum. But what a museum! It's a healthy mixture of classicism and the avant-garde, the latter stunningly exemplified in the Art Nouveau movement, which emerged as the capital licked its wounds in the aftermath of the Commune.

Suddenly, Baron Haussmann's straight-lined architecture felt as rigid as a corset. With Paris entering a new era of peace and economic success, Parisians were in the mood for something a little less strait-laced. Art Nouveau, with its slender curves, was just the ticket, and it wasn't restricted to architecture. The movement embodied the idea that art should be accessible to everyone at all times. There was no need to go to a museum to experience Art Nouveau — *flâneurs* landed upon it by chance, when eating in a brasserie, shopping in a department store, or going to the public lavatory on the place de la Madeleine.

The elegance of Art Nouveau was also applied to street furniture — to lamp-posts, railings and benches — which brought an element of femininity to the capital. Morris columns (named after Gabriel Morris, the Parisian printer who invented them in 1850) were designed for the sole purpose of displaying a brand-new art form — poster art — produced by some of the finest artists of the day, including Toulouse-Lautrec and Alphonse Mucha. The later Art Deco style, which came into being between the two world wars, was another avant-garde movement of which there are many examples in Paris.

Everyone has an opinion about skyscrapers and the Swiss-born French architect Le Corbusier, who is credited with inventing them. In fact, 'Corbu' is the architect opinionated Parisians love to hate. He's often blamed for the functional minimalism of the modern concrete blocks that developers are throwing up all over the city, and for his influence on the construction of cheap high-rise housing. His vision was actually

PREVIOUS PAGES From the Left Bank's Luxembourg Gardens to the Palais Royal's stately courtyards (pictured) on the Right Bank, Paris proffers secret gardens, providing solace from the brouhaha of city life.

ABOVE Typically Parisian Haussmann façades and wrought-iron balconies – a stone's throw from the Musée Nissim de Camondo and its exceptional collection of eighteenth-century furniture and porcelain.

much more subtle, as exemplified by the Swiss pavilion he built for Paris's Cité Universitaire in 1930.

During the 1980s a generation of architects decided to combat 'functionalism for functionalism's sake'. Ricardo Bofill was part of this group, and he proposed neo-neo-classical buildings that 'tell a story' – as in his Montparnasse and Montpellier housing projects.

It's true that Paris has all the richness of a museum, but it's no dusty collection of monuments and buildings – it's very much alive. Leafy green spaces have popped up all over town, some of them perched on top of skyscrapers or railway viaducts, as can be seen in Montparnasse and the 12th arrondissement. The decentralization of major cultural complexes has given previously disadvantaged neighbourhoods a new lease of life. Bercy, the *quartier* where Paris's old wine depots used to be, boasts a rock and sports stadium within walking distance of the Cinémathèque, and also has 'Bercy Village', a village-style commercial centre. On the site of the capital's former abattoirs, La Villette's La Cité des Sciences et de l'Industrie in the 19th arrondissement is a metallic-structured city-within-a-city devoted to experimental arts and technology. It's just a stone's throw from France's top music conservatory,

ABOVE La Villette's La Cité des Sciences et de l'Industrie is a metallic-structured city-within-a-city, designed to inform the public about current developments in arts and technology. Among its high-tech attractions is La Géode, a geodesic sphere housing an Imax cinema.

which houses a state-of-the-art museum of music.

Paris has had a restless history peppered with spectacular incidents, colourful characters and remarkable achievements. At the beginning of the twenty-first century, it faces various challenges, but I also think it has a promising future. As Humphrey Bogart says to Ingrid Bergman in the film *Casablanca* (1942), 'We'll always have Paris'. The aura of the city of enlightenment, style and culture will surely always be with us.

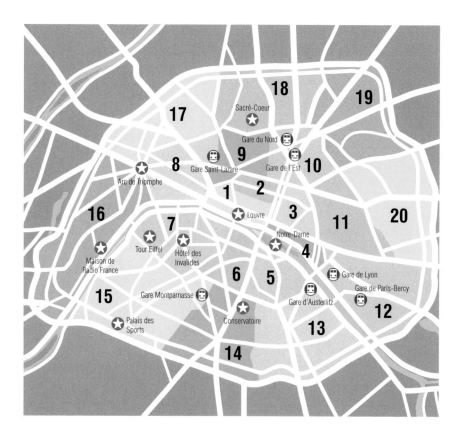

THE ARRONDISSEMENTS

London has boroughs and districts. New York has precincts and neighbourhoods. Paris has quartiers and arrondissements. This can be puzzling for first-time visitors to the capital. Yet, each of these quarters constitutes a piece of the puzzle that defines our city's multi-cultural atmosphere. Just as Londoners relate to their boroughs – mentioning them in passing throughout the day ('I live in Islington', 'I shop in Chelsea', 'I work in Mayfair' and so on) – Parisians are attached to their arrondissements. The name of an arrondissement represents much more to us than an area marked out on a map. As the map shows, they are numbered from one to 20, forming a clockwise spiral, starting with the 1st arrondissement in the heart of the city on the Right Bank to the north of the Seine.

The inhabitants of the 1st arrondissement are lucky. They live next to the Louvre, within walking distance of central Paris's key quarters. For a peek at the Elysée presidential palace or an up-market shopping spree, stroll in the direction of the chic 8th arrondissement. To catch up with the latest developments in contemporary art, head for the Pompidou Centre in the 4th, famous for its medieval Jewish quarter and 'gay Paree' ambience.

Index

Page numbers in *italics* refer to illustrations.

Picture credits

BBC Books would like to thank the following for providing photographs and for permission to use copyright material. While every effort has been made to trace and acknowledge copyright holders, we would like to apologize should there have been any errors or omissions.

Page 1 Corbis/Michel Setboun; 6 (left) Alamy/Hideo Kurihara; 8 British Film Industry/Soda Pictures Ltd; 12 (left) UPPA/Photoshot; 12–13 Corbis Sygma/Alain Nogues; 13 (right) Corbis/Hulton-Deutsch Collection; 14–15 Corbis Sygma; 16 Corbis/Owen Franken; 17 Lauros/Giraudon, Musée de la Ville de Paris, Musée Carnavalet, Paris, France/The Bridgeman Art Library; 19 (top) Corbis/Nathalie Darbellay; 19 (bottom) Corbis/Morton Beebe; 23 Art Directors and Trip/Robin Smith; 26 (left) Corbis/Massimo Listri; 28 (top) Musée de la Ville de Paris, Musée Carnavalet, Paris, France/The Bridgeman Art Library; 28 (bottom) Corbis/Reuters; 31 Agnew's, London, UK, Private Collection/The Bridgeman Art Library; 33 (both) Corbis Sygma/Annebicque Bernard; 36 Corbis/Owen Franken; 37 (top) British Film Institute/MGM; 37 (bottom) Corbis/Bettmann; 39 Getty Images/Iconica; 40 Photoshot/Starstock; 45 Corbis/Yann Arthus-Bertrand; 47 Corbis/Underwood and Underwood; 48–49 By kind permission of Hôtel du Petit Moulin, Paris/Gregoire Korganow; 49 (right) By kind permission of Hôtel de Crillon, Paris; 50 (left) Lauros/Giraudon, Musée de la Ville de Paris, Musée Carnavalet, Paris, France/The Bridgeman Art Library; 52 © Bonhams, London, UK, Phillips, The International Fine Art Auctioneers, UK/The Bridgeman Art Library; 54–5 Corbis/Tibor Bognar; 57 Archives Charmet, Bibliothèque des Arts Decoratifs, Paris, France/The Bridgeman Art Library; 60 Photoshot/World Pictures; 61 Corbis/KUBA; 62 Corbis/Tibor Bognár; 63 (top) De Agostini/World Illustrated/Photoshot; 63 (bottom) Palazzo Pitti, Florence, Italy/The Bridgeman Art Library; 69 (left) Musée Antoine Lecuyer, Saint-Quentin, France/The Bridgeman Art Library; 69 (right) Alte Pinakothek, Munich, Germany/The Bridgeman Art Library; 80–1 Corbis/Bass Museum of Art; 83 Ken Welsh, Private Collection/The Bridgeman Art Library; 85 Corbis/Leonard de Selva; 90 UPPA/Photoshot; 91 (left) Corbis/The Art Archive; 91 (right) Corbis/Burstein Collection; 92–3 Louvre, Paris, France/The Bridgeman Art Library; 95 Corbis/Archivo Iconografico, SA; 100 British Film Institute/Production Companies Films Historiques , Westi, Societe Génerale des Films; 101 AISA/Woodland Illustrated/Photoshot; 102 Musée de la Revolution Française, Vizille, France/The Bridgeman Art Library; 103 Corbis; 106 (top) AKG Images; 106 (bottom) AISA/World Illustrated/Photoshot;

110–11 Giraudon, Louvre, Paris, France/The Bridgeman Art Library; 113 Giraudon, Louvre, Paris, France/The Bridgeman Art Library; 114 Lauros/Giraudon, Louvre, Paris, France/The Bridgeman Art Library; 116 Bibliothèque Nationale, Paris, France/The Bridgeman Art Library; 117 Archives Charmet, Private Collection/The Bridgeman Art Library; 122–3 Corbis/Stefano Bianchetti; 124 Corbis/Bettmann; 125 Art Directors and Trip/Tibor Bognar; 127 Art Directors and Trip/Tibor Bognar; 129 AISA/World Illustrated/Photoshot; 131 (centre) Corbis/Bettmann; 131 (bottom) Photoshot/UPPA; 133 Robert Harding Picture Library/Gavin Hellier; 134 Corbis/Paul Almasy; 135 (top) Corbis/Angelo Hornak; 135 (bottom) Corbis/Robert Holmes; 136 (top) Corbis/Robert Holmes; 136 (bottom) Corbis/Harald A. Jahn; 139 (main image) Photoshot/Starstock; 139 (inset) Private Collection/The Bridgeman Art Library; 141 Corbis/Owen Franken; 142 Corbis/Bettmann; 143 Photoshot/Starstock; 145 (top) National Gallery, London, UK/The Bridgeman Art Library; 146 (left) Alamy/Claude Thibault; 151 (main image) Corbis Sygma/Alain Nogues; 151 (inset) Photoshot/UPPA; 152–3 Corbis/TempSport/Jean-Yves Ruszniewski; 154 Photoshot/Starstock; 155 Starstock/Photoshot; 156 Art Directors and Trip/Richard Drury; 157 (both) Corbis/Bettmann; 160 (left) Corbis/Bettmann; 160 (right) Corbis Sygma/John Bryson; 161 (left) Corbis/Bettmann; 161 (right) Corbis/Underwood and Underwood; 166 Corbis Sygma/Pierre Vauthey; 167 (left) Corbis/Hulton-Deutsch Collection; 167 (right) Photoshot/UPPA; 170–1 Corbis Sygma/Bernard Annebicque; 172 British Film Institute/Arrow Film Distributors Ltd; 173 (top) Corbis Sygma/Patrick Camboulive; 173 (bottom) UPPA/Photoshot; 174 Photoshot/Starstock; 175 (top left) Corbis/Hulton-Deutsch Collection; 175 (top right) Corbis/Bettmann; 175 (bottom left) Corbis/Christie's Images; 175 (bottom centre) ANSA/Starstock/Photoshot; 175 (bottom right) Corbis/Bettmann; 176 (both) Corbis/Condé Nast Archive; 177 (both) Corbis/Condé Nast Archive; 178 (both) Itar-Tass/UPPA/Photoshot; 179 Corbis/Neal Preston; 180 Art Directors and Trip/ASK Images; 181 Photoshot/World Pictures.

Photographs on the following pages © Thibaud Rebour: 5 (top, 2nd and 3rd), 6–7, 9, 21, 18, 24–5, 29, 34, 41, 42–3, 50–1, 58–9, 66–7, 70–1, 73, 76–7, 88, 98–9, 108–9, 119, 126, 131 (top), 132, 138, 148, 149, 158–9, 163, 168–9, 185, 186–7.

Photographs on the following pages © Jeff Eden: 2–3, 4, 5 (bottom), 10–11, 20, 22, 26–7, 48 (left), 53, 74, 86–7, 64–5, 94, 104–5, 121, 146–7, 164–5, 182–3.

This book is published to accompany the television series entitled *Paris*, first broadcast on BBC 2 in 2007.

Executive producer: Kim Thomas

10 9 8 7 6 5 4 3 2 1

Published in 2007 by BBC Books, an imprint of Ebury Publishing.

Ebury Publishing is a division of the Random House Group.

Copyright © Woodlands Books Ltd 2007

The Random House Group Limited
Reg. No. 954009

Addresses for companies within the Random House Group can be found at www.randomhouse.co.uk

A CIP catalogue record for this book is available from the British Library

ISBN 978 0 563 53911 7

The Random House Group Limited makes every effort to ensure that the papers used in our books are made from trees that have been legally sourced from well-managed and credibly certified forests. Our paper procurement policy can be found at www.randomhouse.co.uk

Commissioning editors:
Vivien Bowler and Martin Redfern
Project editor: Christopher Tinker
Copy-editors: Patricia Burgess and Tessa Clark
Designer: Andrew Barron
Picture researcher: Joanne Forrest-Smith
Production controller: Kenneth McKay

Printed and bound by Firmengruppe APPL, aprinta druck, Wemding, Germany